CBoyle

July '97

GW01191958

**Pluto Handbooks**

Nathalie Hadjifotiou

# Women and Harassment at Work

Pluto  Press

First published in 1983 by Pluto Press Limited,
The Works, 105a Torriano Avenue, London NW5 2RX
and Pluto Press Australia Ltd, PO Box 199, Leichhardt,
New South Wales 2040, Australia

Copyright © Nathalie Hadjifotiou, 1983

Text designed by Claudine Meissner
Cover designed by Colin Bailey
Photoset by Wayside Graphics, Clevedon, Avon
Printed in Great Britain by St. Edmundsbury Press,
Bury St. Edmunds, Suffolk
Bound by Garden City Press, Letchworth, Herts

British Library Cataloguing in Publication Data
Hadjifotiou, Nathalie
    Women and harassment at work.
    1. Sexual harassment of women – Great Britain
    2. Women – Employment – Great Britain
    I. Title
    306.7      HD6060.3

ISBN 0-86104-729-X

# Contents

**Preface** v

**Introduction** 1
Why harassment is a workplace issue 1
Taking up the issue 2
About the book 3

**Part 1: The issue** 5

**1. What is sexual harassment?** 7
Definitions 8
Evidence 9
Examples 13
Consequences of sexual harassment 18
Explaining sexual harassment at work 23
Summary 25

**2. Women at work** 27
Sexism at work 28
Traditional women's work 40
Working in a man's world 45
Positive action 53

**Part 2: Taking action** 57

**3. Individual action** 59
Avoiding harassment 60
Getting support 61
Keeping a written record 62
Complaining 63
Retaliating 65
Contacting women's groups 66
Assertiveness and self-defence training 67

**4. Organising in the unions** 69
Sexism within trade unions 70
Trade-union policies 75
Workplace procedures 78
Organising for women 82
Helping men understand sexism 85
Education and training 87

**5. Workplace campaigns**                                    96
Campaigning against pin-ups                                   99
Workplace questionnaires                                     107
Meetings                                                     122
Publicity                                                    125

**6. Collective agreements**                                  130
Negotiating arguments                                        132
Management policies                                          133
Training programme                                           139
Procedures for handling complaints                           141

**7. Using the law**                                          148
Relevant law                                                 149
Sexual harassment as sex discrimination                      150
Sexual harassment and unfair dismissal                       157
Health and safety at work                                    161
Using the criminal and civil courts                          162
Making a claim under the Sex Discrimination Act              166
Making a claim for unfair dismissal                          180
Legal advice                                                 180

Useful addresses                                             183

Bibliography                                                 185

Index                                                        188

# Preface

Time, as everyone knows, moves on. I started writing this handbook in October 1982. It was finished the following June. By the time it is published, thousands more women will have been sexually harassed at work; some will have quit, others resigned themselves to a lifetime of humiliation. But women have also found the strength to fight back. A number of tribunal cases may be heard over the next few months. Unions are drawing up policies for tackling sexual harassment in response to members' demands. Women are learning self-defence.

Collecting together the various accounts of workplace activities has been frustrating, frightening and exciting. Frustrating, because so much information remains confidential for fear of jeopardising a negotiation or court hearing. Frightening, because as yet there is little evidence of the long-term success of any workplace initiative in changing the attitudes and behaviour of men. Exciting, because the experiences of women and men actively campaigning against sexism at work, illustrated in this handbook, show how much activity is already taking place to change men's views of working women.

The information in this handbook should not be read as a blueprint for automatic success. With campaigning against sexual harassment at work still in its infancy, there are as yet few tried and trusted remedies. There is no right way to go about removing pin-ups, or altering the language men use when talking to women. I set out to convince readers that sexism and sexual harassment seriously restrict women's employment opportunities and undermine their value and status as workers. I want to show that this situation is not inevitable but can be changed by active campaigning within the workplace. I want to give women experiencing harassment information and encouragement to do something about it. And I am concerned to provide readers with practical ideas for action so that they can start a workplace campaign with some knowledge of the problems and possibilities involved. Hopefully, readers will generate their own ideas, as well as adapting activities in this handbook, to fit their own working environment.

Hang on a minute! Could all this talk of removing sexual harassment from the workplace simply be the vision of a utopian dreamer? For several years I was active with other women to provide refuge for women beaten up by the men they live with. Despite 10 years of campaigning, refuges remain full, violence continues. Little in our society supports women fighting to combat sexism. Schools continue to treat boys and girls differently; the media portrays women as passive, simpering fools; the lack of an adequate income makes women financially dependent on men; pornography presents an image of women as sex objects, existing to satisfy the power and lust of men. With this cultural background, many might argue that campaigning against sexual harassment at work has about as much chance of success as Canute's bid to control the waves.

I would not have written the handbook if I did not believe in the possibility of changing the traditional relationship between women and men. Challenging sexual harassment at work is a small, but essential part of that fight. Already in my lifetime working women have secured important advances. Just 20 years ago there was no paid maternity leave or the right for women to return to work after having a baby; 10 years ago no one would have predicted a TUC march in support of the right of women to have an abortion; five years ago there was no interest from unions in negotiating special measures to improve women's opportunities at work. Small as these changes sometimes appear, they have been won by many thousands of campaigning initiatives in workplaces across the country. Sexual harassment at work has now reached the top of the agenda.

This handbook brings together information, experiences and ideas of many people and organisations, concerned about sexual harassment at work. I would like to thank Andy Carty, Gill Coates, Ruth Elliot, George Hickman, Judith Hunt, Carole Leathwood, Angela Mason, Hilary Matthews, Vicky Rosin and Anne Sedley for information about specific issues and campaigns. A number of trade unions replied to my enquiries about their policy towards sexual harassment at work, including the TUC Women's Advisory Committee, ASTMS, CPSA, GMBATU, IPCS, NALGO, SCPS, TASS and UCATT. Particular thanks are due to Sandwell Joint Shop Stewards Committee and NALGO branches in Liverpool and Camden for enabling me to publish details of their workplace campaigns. Other contributing organisations were Leeds TUCRIC, the Equal Opportunities Commission and the Institute of Personnel Managers. Thanks also to the Alfred Marks Bureau for permission to publish their survey findings and to Sue Read for letting me quote extensively from her book *Sexual Harassment at Work*.

Finally, this handbook would not have been written without the support and encouragement of Tess Woodcraft. Her close involvement with the project ranged from playing a major part in the primary planning to reading and commenting on the final manuscript. Much of the initial material for the handbook arose from her own campaigning on sexual harassment at work. I, of course, take full responsibility for the final content, including any errors both of fact and interpretation. A book which talks about people's feelings and attitudes almost inevitably reflects the author's own view of the world; this handbook is no exception. In raising an unpleasant and distressing aspect of women's working lives, I am hopeful that both women and men will recognise the need and have the confidence to do something about it.

# Introduction

In 1980 Vicky Stevans, a typist with a Midlands company, won a claim for unfair dismissal after she was sacked for complaining about her employer's offensive behaviour. A year later, two other women who had both experienced sexual advances at work were awarded compensation for their subsequent losses of job. And in 1982 a survey published by the Alfred Marks Bureau showed 60 per cent of participating employees had received unwelcome sexual attention from people they worked with. Hidden for so long, the sexual harassment of working women is at last becoming recognised as a genuine workplace problem.

Today, women are beginning to talk about their experiences of sexual harassment at work. There is increasing concern not only about ways of tackling individual cases when they arise but also over how to challenge traditional working relationships which foster sexism and the harassment of women at work. This handbook aims to give workers practical guidance on:

- **the forms of sexual harassment experienced by women workers;**
- **how workers are affected by harassment;**
- **the impact of harassment on women's employment opportunities;**
- **how to tackle individual problems at work;**
- **trade-union policies on harassment and sexism at work;**
- **workplace campaigns to identify and combat harassment;**
- **management approaches to dealing with sexual harassment;**
- **negotiating collective agreements on harassment.**

## Why harassment is a workplace issue

Sexual harassment at work is an important issue for women. The personal suffering and injury resulting from harassment is an aspect of working life that women share with very few men.

However, the impact of harassment extends beyond the individual experiences of particular women and affects the working conditions of women generally.

To date, the Equal Pay Act and the Sex Discrimination Act have failed to significantly improve employment opportunities for women. Sexual harassment **reinforces a view of women as playthings and sex objects**, creatures which neither employer nor male co-worker take seriously. Unless these attitudes change, demands from women for better pay, equal opportunities and positive action programmes may well fall on deaf ears.

For trade unions, sexual harassment raises basic aspects of **working conditions**. Any worker experiencing stress, deteriorating health, absenteeism, dismissal, disciplinary action or other forms of victimisation expects the support of their trade union. But when these consequences for women arise as a result of harassment, they may go unrecognised because the harassment either remains **hidden** or is considered an **unquestioned and natural part of working life**.

## Taking up the issue

It is only recently that sexual harassment at work has been recognised as a legitimate workplace grievance. The first cases to gain publicity were in the USA when several women took action under the equal opportunities law. Subsequently women's groups and trade unions in Canada and Australia, as well as the USA, began raising the issue. In 1980 the European Commission (the civil service of the Common Market) undertook a survey to highlight the problem in a number of countries, including Britain.

In Britain, women have begun to raise the issue of sexual harassment within the trade-union movement. Both at local and national level there are the beginnings of an awareness that trade-union action is needed to overcome sexism and harassment at the workplace. The TUC has issued guidelines on the issue. Women trade-union members are getting together to support women who are victims of harassment; many have been encouraged to speak out about their experiences after years of fear and distress.

Women's groups and organisations involved in campaigns about violence and the sexist attitudes women face in their everyday lives also offer support for victims of sexual harassment. Conferences, workshops and discussion groups have been held in many parts of the country. The industrial tribunal cases mentioned earlier have given the problem of sexual harassment added publicity.

## About the book

The ability of workers to tackle sexual harassment in their workplaces is seriously hampered by the invisibility and normality of sexist attitudes and harassment at work. Part 1 of the handbook sets out to **establish the significance of harassment** as a negative feature of women's working lives. Chapter 1 looks at the **evidence** for treating sexual harassment as a serious problem. Using examples from a range of work situations, it illustrates how workers can identify practices and attitudes in their workplace which enable harassment to flourish. Chapter 2 examines the **critical role** of sexual harassment in reinforcing the inferior status of women at work. The handbook argues that achieving major changes in women's pay and working conditions is dependent on challenging sexist attitudes and practices in the workplace.

Part 2 examines various **ways of tackling** sexual harassment at work. Many women are employed in small, unorganised workplaces, work part-time or flexible hours, and are paid to perform a range of services for male workers – as, for example, secretaries, shop assistants and cleaners. Under these circumstances women workers are often **isolated and vulnerable**, and taking action against harassment presents particular difficulties. Chapter 3 explores some of the ways which can be tried to stop harassment in situations where there is a **lack of workplace organisation or support from co-workers**.

While taking action against an individual harasser may remove an immediate problem, it does little to alter the working environment which encourages such practices. Women workers are concerned that trade unions take up the broader question of sexist attitudes and behaviour, not only in the workplace but also within their own trade union. Chapter 4 examines current **trade-union approaches** to the issue and includes suggestions for branch and workplace activity. Chapter 5 outlines the **practical experiences** and advice of trade unionists who have campaigned around sexism and harassment in their workplaces. It gives practical guidance for groups of workers wanting to start a campaign in their workplace.

Not only trade unions but also managements are becoming

aware of their responsibilities to tackle harassment at work. Some employers are reviewing their **workplace policies and procedures** for dealing with sexual harassment, in part to limit any liability they may have for the actions of their employees. Chapter 6 describes a number of these management guidelines and suggests ways in which trade unions may wish to amend or introduce **collective agreements** to offer women workers greater protection.

Finally, chapter 7 examines ways in which **the law** may help a worker who leaves her job or is discriminated against because of harassment. While none of the legal options is very satisfactory, there is increasing interest in how the Sex Discrimination Act might be used to support victims of harassment. The handbook discusses this as well as briefly outlining the possible use of other legal remedies.

The information in the handbook is drawn from a wide range of organisations and individuals actively involved in challenging sexism and harassment at work. Lists of **useful contacts** and **further reading** are included at the end of the handbook. The practical experiences from these sources illustrate ways in which workers can tackle the issue. Given the short time which has elapsed since the first cases of sexual harassment hit the headlines, it is impossible to indicate how successful any of them will be in reducing and eventually removing harassment from the workplace. In using the handbook, readers will need to consider the circumstances of their own workplace and decide how best to adapt and develop the various activities.

Finally, not everyone who picks up this handbook will start by agreeing with all its contents. The information should be of use to many women since it is they who experience sexual harassment. Because men harass women, male readers may fear the book points too accusing a finger in their direction. It is important that everyone is aware of the consequences of behaviour which many women find distressing and which is often harmful. But the aim of the handbook is not to make men feel guilty; rather to help all workers recognise that taken-for-granted attitudes and behaviour help to **maintain the disadvantage and discrimination of women at work**. Having critically examined the day-to-day life of their workplace, anyone concerned to take effective action against sexism and sexual harassment will hopefully find the handbook useful.

# Part 1:
## The issue

# 1.

# What is sexual harassment?

Definitions / evidence / examples / consequences / explanations / summary.

Sexual harassment of women at work is not new. Enquiries into the working conditions in Britain during the mid-nineteenth century reported time and again physical and sexual abuse suffered by both women and children. Evidence from the 1832–4 Poor Law Commission prompted Frederick Engels to write:

> The employer is sovereign over the persons and charms of his employees. The threat of discharge suffices to overcome all resistance in nine cases out of ten . . . If the master is mean enough, and the official report mentions several such cases, his mill is also his harem; the fact that not all manufacturers use their power does not in the least change the position of the girls. (Engels, p. 177)

Similar incidents were recorded in the USA. A shop girl wrote to the Jewish daily *Forward* in 1907 after she had lost her job because she refused the foreman's advances:

> The girls in the shop were very upset by the foreman's vulgarity but they didn't want him to throw them out, so they are afraid to be witnesses against him. What can be done about this? (Bularzik, p. 8.)

In 1980, national newspapers in Britain reported the case of a clerk with a small builders' merchants who left her job because of her boss's behaviour. He touched her up, played with her clothing, and talked about their going away for the weekend.

Little appears to have changed in the seventy-odd years separating these incidents. There is, however, a difference. The shop girl in 1907 was left to fend for herself; the clerk took her case to an industrial tribunal and was awarded £945 compensation for unfair dismissal. While in no way making up for the humiliation and job loss she suffered, it was a victory of sorts. Sexual harassment at work, so long taken for granted as a natural part of working life, is becoming recognised as a serious problem for women.

## Definitions

What is sexual harassment? Organisations campaigning on the issue have produced a number of definitions. The *TUC Guidelines* state:

> A broad definition of sexual harassment would include repeated and unwanted verbal or sexual advances, sexually explicit derogatory statements or sexually discriminating remarks which are offensive to the worker involved, which cause the worker to feel threatened, humiliated, patronised or harassed or which interfere with the worker's job performance, undermine job security or create a threatening or intimidating work environment. Sexual harassment can take many forms, from leering, ridicule, embarrassing remarks or jokes, unwelcome comments about dress or appearance, deliberate abuse, the repeated and/or unwanted physical contact, demands for sexual favours, or physical assaults on workers.

How sexual harassment **interferes with the victim's job performance** is detailed by the Health and Research Employees Association of Australia:

> Any physical or verbal conduct of a sexual nature constitutes sexual harassment when:
> (i) it is unsolicited, repeated and unwelcome; or
> (ii) when submission to such conduct is implicitly or explicitly a term or condition of an individual's employment; or
> (iii) when submission to such conduct is implicitly or explicitly a term or condition for decisions which would affect promotion, salary or any other job condition; or
> (iv) when such behaviour creates an intimidating, hostile or offensive work environment for one or more employees.

Other definitions recognise that the **majority of harassers are men and their victims women:** 'Sexual harassment is unsolicited, non-reciprocal male behaviour that asserts a woman's sex role over her function as a worker.' (Farley, p. 33.) Such a definition broadens the issue beyond the problem of individuals to encompass the idea that sexual harassment is behaviour experienced by women **simply because they are women**. Thus harassment involves not only the more obvious forms of sexual abuse but a wide range of attitudes and behaviour which are commonplace at work.

Sexual harassment is any unwanted attention of a sexual nature from someone from the workplace that creates discomfort and/or interferes with the job . . . Sexual harassment is not limited to a single incident of molestation or threats that failure to comply with a supervisor's sexual demands will result in firing. It includes a work environment laden with sex-stereotyped attitudes and behaviour which emphasises a woman's sexuality and denigrates her role as a worker. (Working Woman's Institute, New York.)

Drawing together the elements of these various definitions, the handbook will use the term sexual harassment to mean **all those actions and practices by a person or group of people at work which are directed at one or more workers and which:**

- **are repeated and unwanted;**
- **may be deliberate or done unconsciously;**
- **cause humiliation, offence or distress;**
- **may interfere with job performance or create an unpleasant working environment;**
- **comprise remarks or actions associated with a person's sex;**
- **emphasise a person's sexuality over her role as a worker.**

# Evidence

Over the last few years, a number of surveys have been carried out to identify both the extent and nature of sexual harassment at work. The most detailed have taken place in the USA, since concern over the issue developed earlier there than in Britain. In 1976 a woman's magazine, *Redbook*, published a questionnaire to find out how women coped with unwanted sexual advances at work. They received 9,000 replies, with **nine out of ten** women reporting experiences of sexual harassment at work. The same questions were used to collate evidence from women living at a Californian naval base and nearby town; **81 per cent** of women surveyed had experienced some form of sexual harassment.

At the United Nations, the Ad Hoc Group on the Equal Rights for Women Committee polled the female employees; **50 per cent** reported incidents of harassment. In March 1981, the US Merit Systems Protection Board published the findings of a major survey of 20,314 federal government employees. Of women employees, **42 per cent** had experienced harassment.

## Table 1: Percentage of women federal employees who experienced each form of harassment (US Merit Systems Protection Board, 1981)

| | |
|---|---|
| Sexual remarks | 33 |
| Suggestive looks | 28 |
| Deliberate touching | 26 |
| Pressure for dates | 15 |
| Pressure for sexual favours | 9 |
| Letters and calls | 9 |
| Actual or attempted rape | 1 |

Surveys in Britain have, to date, been more limited in scope. In January 1982 the Alfred Marks Bureau surveyed 799 employees and managers who use their 'temp' agency. Women accounted for 82 per cent of employees and 65 per cent of managers; 66 per cent of employees and 86 per cent of managers were aware of the problem of sexual harassment. More than **60 per cent** of employees had themselves experienced harassment at least once; 17 per cent had been harassed more than six times in their working life. The harassment experienced by British women managers has been documented by Cooper and Davidson in their book *High Pressure*. Of the small number of women managers questioned, **54 per cent** said they had experienced some form of harassment, particularly women in lower and middle management posts.

The incidence of sexual harassment in individual workplaces has been recorded by surveys of local government. Two branches of NALGO, in Liverpool and Camden (London), approached their members for information. In Camden, **163 women out of 514** reported experiences of harassment at their present workplace, and a further 196 reported incidents at a previous workplace. In Liverpool, of the 179 questionnaires returned, **98** indicated incidents of harassment, more than half of which related to their current workplace.

These surveys show clearly that a significant number of women are victims of sexual harassment at work. Questionnaires

## Table 2: What employees and managers think constitutes sexual harassment (Alfred Marks Bureau, 1982)

| | Possibly harassment | | Sexual harassment | |
| | Employees % | Management % | Employees % | Management % |
|---|---|---|---|---|
| Being eyed up and down | 29 | 26 | 4 | 2 |
| Suggestive looks at parts of the body | 53 | 56 | 20 | 10 |
| Regular sexual remarks/jokes | 48 | 56 | 17 | 13 |
| Cheek kissing on meeting or parting | 27 | 30 | 13 | 8 |
| Being asked out on dates despite refusing | 43 | 51 | 36 | 33 |
| Touching or patting | 44 | 63 | 42 | 22 |
| Pinching or grabbing | 24 | 26 | 75 | 73 |
| Direct sexual proposition | 13 | 20 | 82 | 80 |
| Forcible sexual aggression | 3 | 1 | 94 | 98 |

identified very few cases of men being harassed by women. The figures confirm what women themselves have always known – that sexual harassment at work is **almost exclusively practised by men and directed at women**. It is an established part of women's working lives. Certain types of sexual behaviour were recognised in all the surveys as forms of harassment – **sexual assault, demands for sex, touching and pinching, crude sexual remarks and persistent demands for dates**. There was some difference of view about including other forms of sexist behaviour. Nevertheless, a variety of other actions were indentified as possible causes of harassment – **being eyed up and down, kissed on the cheek, flirting and sexual jokes**.

## Table 3: Types of harassment experienced by women at their present workplace (NALGO: Camden Branch Survey, unpublished)

| | |
|---|---|
| Staring or leering | 70 |
| Sexual remarks or teasing | 154 |
| Touching, brushing against, grabbing | 69 |
| Other more serious forms of sexual assault | 5 |

How far a group of workers view a particular form of behaviour as harassment will depend, to some extent, on their own experiences and awareness of the problem. Managers, particularly those in more senior positions, are less likely to consider harassment an issue because they are isolated from the majority of their workers. Women, since they are more likely than men to experience harassment, tend to identify a broader range of behaviour as offensive or distressing. The *Harvard Business Review* asked its readers whether they agreed that the amount of sexual harassment at work is greatly exaggerated. While 66 per cent of men agreed, only 32 per cent of women did so. Of top management, 63 per cent considered the statement correct, compared to only 44 per cent of lower management.

One issue examined by some surveys is the difference in response if the harasser is a supervisor rather than a co-worker. Because of the control which a supervisor exercises over a worker's job prospects, harassment from a superior was **usually viewed more seriously**. The *Harvard Business Review* survey records only 20 per cent of respondents including persistent requests for dates by a co-worker as harassment, but 46 per cent considered it harassment if a supervisor was involved. Similar results were recorded by the US Merit Systems Protection Board; 91 per cent of women said deliberate touching by a superior was

## Table 4: Views of respondents on what constitutes sexual harassment (Collins and Blodgett, 1981)

|  | Definitely % | Possibly % |
|---|---|---|
| Patted or pinched by boss | 90 | 8 |
| Agree to dates for good of career | 79 | 17 |
| Have sex for good of career | 78 | 20 |
| Demotion following break-up of affair | 87 | 7 |
| Eyed up and down: by supervisor | 16 | 60 |
| by co-worker | 15 | 54 |
| Sexual remarks: from supervisor | 44 | 46 |
| from co-worker | 37 | 49 |
| Frequently glanced at: by supervisor | 1 | 26 |
| by co-worker | 2 | 26 |
| Kiss on cheek at meeting: supervisor | 46 | 43 |
| co-worker | 20 | 47 |
| Persistent asking for dates: supervisor | 48 | 39 |
| co-worker | 20 | 41 |
| Hand on arm when making a point: supervisor | 3 | 44 |
| co-worker | 4 | 42 |

harassment, whereas for a co-worker the proportion dropped to 84 per cent. Counter to this the Alfred Marks Bureau recorded 11 per cent of respondents as being more tolerant of sexual approaches by a boss or more senior member of staff, a figure they considered surprisingly low having regard to the high rate of unemployment.

These variations in the assessment of both the degree and forms of harassment have important implications for tackling the issue in the workplace. Convincing many workers that there is a problem is a very necessary first step. What these surveys reveal is:

- **a large number of workers are victims of sexual harassment at work;**
- **almost all the victims are women and the harassers are men;**
- **a wide range of behaviour is identified by many workers as harassment;**
- **the way workers view the problem of sexual harassment depends on their own awareness and experiences of the issue;**
- **lower management are more aware of the problem than higher management;**
- **harassment by a supervisor is viewed as more serious than by a co-worker.**

## Examples

Statistical surveys are a useful summary of the general incidence of and attitudes towards sexual harassment. A set of figures, however, cannot convey as clearly as their own words the experiences and feelings of women subjected to such behaviour. Not unnaturally, victims are reluctant to speak openly for fear of public humiliation and retaliation at work. The cases mentioned here represent the more obvious forms of harassment, where most women suffered serious distress. Much of the run-of-the-mill harassment which undermines self-confidence and operates as a constant reminder of women's 'inferiority' is so subtle and insidious that specific instances go unrecorded.

**Sexual remarks, jokes, catcalls, whistling and teasing** are commonplace at work. It is often difficult for people who are not at the receiving end to understand the extent to which such behaviour is distressing and demeaning; after all, it is only meant in fun. But personal remarks about parts of the body, particularly legs, breasts and hair, along with whistles and catcalls, all serve to remind women that they are judged by their looks rather than their work.

■ **Example:** My boss is incapable of having a meeting or discussion with me without some comment about my sex. There are constant references to the fact you are a woman, your dress, etc., and remarks such as 'you're looking attractive today' or 'I know you will be able to influence so and so by fluttering your eyelashes'. I try to ignore it. (Woman manager; Cooper and Davidson, p. 72.)

When a group of male workers together operate such forms of behaviour, the work environment may appear hostile and threatening. Verbal harassment reinforces the superior position which most men hold in the workplace.

■ **Example:** Women library staff at the *Financial Times* travel a long devious route to deliver files to journalists in the reporters' room. The detour is specifically to avoid the smutty, sexual remarks in the messenger section of the newsroom. (*Natsopa Journal.*)

Because these forms of harassment are such a 'natural' and pervasive part of working life for women and men, they are both the most difficult and perhaps the most important to tackle.

**Sexually explicit materials**, in the form of magazines, promotion calendars, or pin-up photographs from the daily newspapers can be found in thousands of workplaces across the country. Usually they are not displayed with any conscious intention of distressing women; they are just a part of the widespread use of women's bodies in advertising and the cinema. Nevertheless, they carry subtle messages which few women fail to recognise. By depicting women as sexual playthings, creatures engaged in pleasing men, the important skills and responsibilities which women carry out in the workplace are ignored and undervalued. And by offering only one view of the 'perfect woman', pin-ups and girlie calendars undermine women's self-confidence in their own bodies and appearance.

■ **Example:** I felt humiliated every time I came into work and saw this picture of a woman with her legs wide open, looking passive and provocative. I felt it reflected on me, my work status, even my ability to do my job. (Sedley and Benn, p. 97.)

It is not perhaps surprising that some women feel the only way to gain recognition at work is to play up to the images of these pictures. In some cases, maybe where women have commented or complained about pin-ups, this display of offensive material develops into an overt attempt by men in the workplace to humiliate and harass women. Material is deliberately left so it will be seen, sexist and pornographic graffiti may appear on noticeboards and notepads – a clear warning that women who work are in a man's world.

- **Example:** They began by bringing *Playboy* magazine into work and leaving it lying around open, and little sexual drawings began appearing scribbled in my desk diary. Eventually I complained and was moved to another job. (Laboratory technician; Read, p.71.)

**Suggestive looks and gestures, staring and leering** are actions designed to make a woman aware she is the object of sexual interest. Persistent and unwanted behaviour of this kind is disturbing and threatening because at work there is little or no immediate escape. By forcing this kind of attention on a woman, the harasser is demanding to be noticed. Women in this situation cannot win – ignoring the behaviour carries a risk of the harasser increasing his attentions; acknowledging his interest may be taken as tacit acceptance of it. Complaining is difficult if the harasser has power over the woman's job.

- **Example:** Her boss would make her feel uncomfortable by making sexual gestures, he would often lean against her, immobilising her between his own body and the chair. He would never look her in the eyes but instead move his eyes up and down her body below the neck. He would also stand with his hands in his pockets as if rubbing his genitals. (Farley, p. 116.)

**Persistent demands for dates and sexual favours** from a supervisor or co-worker are other ways in which a woman is made aware she is regarded as a sexual being rather than a worker. Direct questions and comments of this sort cannot be easily ignored. It may be particularly difficult to convince the harasser that his attentions are unwanted because women are supposed to be flattered by them. Rejection or avoidance of the harasser may simply be used to fuel the myth that women 'like to play hard to get'. And because a particular woman is picked out for special treatment, she can become isolated within the workplace. Her only option may be to leave.

■ **Example:** He [the male nursing officer] started visiting me when I was alone on night duty. He started nagging me to have an affair with him, a night out, an afternoon, just half an hour. I confided in two of my female colleagues because I didn' know what to do. One of them said I was probably enjoying i and the other thought I should have it off with him and get i over with. Why should I be so humiliated and spend my time dreading his nightly visits to my ward? Why should I have to consider changing my job because of his behaviour? (Nigh nurse; Read, p. 44.)

■ **Example:** A woman who worked for a firm of theatrical cos tumiers left after three months because her boss made her life intolerable. He put his hand up her skirt, grabbed at her and offered her pearls if she would sleep with him. When she rejected him, he gave her less interesting work to do. (Sedley and Benn, p. 6.)

In this case, where harassment involved an employer, outrigh rejection of his advances had direct consequences for the woman's job prospects. Even if retaliation does not happen, the fear that it might remains.

**Touching, pinching, caressing and hugging** all involve physi-cal contact with a woman which under other circumstances could be classed as assault. A criminal prosecution could result from such an incident happening between strangers in the street. At work, people know each other and want to work in a pleasan environment. A familiar excuse for touching and hugging is tha it demonstrates friendship; but unwanted and repeated touching of breasts, buttocks, hair, cannot be mistaken for genuine con cern for a woman's well-being. Manhandling a woman reflects the view, whether consciously or not, that women's bodies are available to men.

■ **Example:** At the end of a social event I was harassed by a vice-president of the company. This included stroking my buttocks and continually rubbing himself against me. I finally managed to get rid of him. For several weeks afterwards he kept calling me. When I found another job, I left. (Compute specialist; Collins and Blodgett, p. 77.)

Most workplaces have areas where women can be trapped on their own – lifts, cloakrooms, dark corridors, an office. While some can be avoided, a request to fetch something from the stores cannot be ignored.

■ **Example:** Well, he comes up to me and traps me in a corner of this deep-freeze and starts touching my tits and bum. I just made a hell of a lot of noise, I was petrified. A couple of days later he told me it was too embarrassing to have me around and I was fired. (Kitchen helper; Read, p. 67.)

Even less obvious sexual approaches, like a hand on the arm or shoulder, imply proprietorial rights over a woman. Such actions, accompanied, for example, by demands from a supervisor to undertake a particular task, are a reminder that the supervisor has power over the woman's job. As a result, such behaviour can be as threatening as more overt forms of harassment.

**Violent sexual assault, rape and attempted rape** do happen at work. Occasionally they are reported to the police but proving a case can be difficult.

■ **Example:** She was a 27-year-old dentist's receptionist. She had worked for this man for about two months. He had chased her round the office, pushed her against the wall and tried to make penetration. She was injured and bleeding vaginally. Of course, the fact is the dentist was not arrested. There was no proof; it was his word against hers. (Farley, p. 21.)

While such cases account for a very small proportion of sexual harassment at work, they are significant because they are a reminder of the physical power which men can exercise over women. The ever-present possibility of violent sexual abuse is a powerful influence over how women react to other forms of harassment. On the one hand there is the fear that resisting sexual advances may provoke violent assault and rape so it is safer to comply; at the same time there is a feeling of thankfulness that this particular approach was not as bad as it might have been – a feeling which stops women from making a complaint. All these examples clearly illustrate that:

● **women experience a wide range of behaviour as sexual harassment;**
● **women in all types of jobs and workplaces experience harassment;**

- most women find such behaviour humiliating and distressing;
- women feel they have to deal with the problem themselves;
- the possibilities of retaliation make it difficult to know what action to take.

## Consequences of sexual harassment

These case studies highlight the lack of effective action by both employers and workers to deal with sexual harassment at work. Far from treating harassment as a serious workplace problem, **its continuation is supported by a number of myths:**

- **Myth 1:** Sexual harassment is nothing more than the **normal and natural** sexual interest existing between women and men. If they work together, innocent flirtation is inevitable.
- **Myth 2:** Women **like to be flattered** about their appearance and expect the men they work with to take notice of them.
- **Myth 3:** Work needs to be brightened up by a few **jokes and games**. Women who do not appreciate a laugh are spoilsports or suffer from sexual inhibitions.
- **Myth 4:** Women who are harassed have **clearly asked for it** by the way they dress and behave. Any woman who is not interested can easily say so.
- **Myth 5:** If women are harassed, it is only those with **personal problems** who are unable to deal with the situation themselves.

As a consequence of these myths, victims of sexual harassment may feel **guilty** about their reactions to behaviour that other people consider trivial, and **ashamed** to tell anyone in case they are blamed for encouraging the harasser. Fear of embarrassment and humiliation from co-workers or an employer can be as or more distressing than the incident itself, and prevents women from speaking out.

Yet the evidence all points to the seriousness of harassment as a cause for concern. Campaigning against sexism and harassment in the workplace is not about limiting sexual freedom and returning to outmoded standards of morality but about **creating a work environment where women do not suffer discrimination and hardship because of their sex**. A clear distinction can be drawn between friendly attention reciprocated by the other person and unwanted and unpleasant behaviour which causes distress and fear. Because of the accepted attitude that sexual harassment is not a problem, **workplace procedures for dealing with particular incidents are inadequate**. Women have to cope on their own as best they can. Some idea of their feelings and actions can be gained from the various surveys.

## Table 5: Feelings of women who experienced harassment (NALGO: Camden Branch Survey, unpublished)

|  | Number |
| --- | --- |
| It was unimportant | 54 |
| It made me feel embarrassed | 74 |
| It made me feel angry | 154 |

## Table 6: Actions taken to protect themselves from harassment (NALGO: Camden Branch Survey, unpublished)

|  | Number |
| --- | --- |
| Pretend not to notice | 101 |
| Adopt a cool, guarded manner | 185 |
| Respond angrily | 87 |

The commonest reactions are:

- to suppress inner feelings and try to ignore it;
- to take time off work;
- to transfer to another job;
- to leave the job;
- to complain and risk retaliation;
- to go along with the harassment for fear of retaliation.

By far the most usual response is **to try and ignore** the harassment in the hope that it will eventually go away. In fact, as one survey quoted by Farley recorded, in **75 per cent of the cases when harassment was ignored it eventually worsened**. Despite a cool, unruffled outward appearance, most victims experience anger, frustration and embarrassment. Respondents to the Alfred Marks Bureau survey reported reactions such as 'nervous, defensive, emotional, discontent, fear and anger'. Because women are expected to be 'unstable', such feelings may not be associated b<sup>.</sup> the employer or co-workers with incidents of harassment. A significant number of victims identified by the US Merit System Protection Board experienced a worsening of their working live and their attitude to the job.

### Table 7: Action taken following an incident as reported by the victim (Alfred Marks Bureau, 1982)

|  | Percentage |
| --- | --- |
| Victim changed jobs | 53 |
| Reported to company but no action taken | 30 |
| Culprit was disciplined | 18 |
| Culprit was dismissed | — |
| Internal transfer of either party | 5 |
| Other | 13 |

### Table 8: Aspects of women workers' lives which 'became worse' as a result of harassment (US Merit Systems Protection Board, 1981)

|  | Percentage |
| --- | --- |
| Feelings about work | 36 |
| Emotional or physical condition | 33 |
| Ability to work with others | 15 |
| Time and attendance at work | 11 |
| The quantity of work done | 11 |
| The quality of work done | 10 |

Psychological and physical reactions, depression, insomnia headaches, all indicate that **harassment is a major contributor t** **stress at work**. The long-term damage to the health and persona well-being of people affected by work-related stress is wel documented:

- decrease in job performance and job satisfaction;
- absenteeism;
- anxiety, tension, irritation, depression;
- increased alcohol, cigarette and drug use;
- sleeplessness and tiredness;
- problems with weight and diet;
- migraine;

- coronary heart disease;
- difficulties with family and personal relationships;
- physical and mental illness.

When harassment becomes unbearable, women take action to remove themselves from the harasser by having days off, asking to be transferred to another section or leaving the job. Over half the victims reported by the Alfred Marks Bureau survey changed jobs, although only 19 out of 62 actually gave harassment as their reason for resigning. Many of the case studies quoted earlier indicate how frequently women see a change of job as the only option. Even where the initial response is to try and ignore it, many women eventually feel compelled to leave.

Victims pay a double penalty for, in addition to being harassed, changing or transferring jobs can have a **negative effect on long-term job prospects**. Promotion, seniority and sick pay, pension rights and opportunities for training are frequently linked to length of service. Forced to sacrifice these benefits, victims of harassment help justify the view that women are not interested in job or career opportunities. And the widely held assumption that women are unreliable workers is confirmed by poor job performance, absenteeism, requests for transfer without obvious reasons and an unwillingness to work after normal hours. As a consequence, harassment not only affects individual women workers but **contributes to the unsatisfactory overall conditions which women experience within the job market**.

**The negative costs of harassment affect employers** as well as workers. The US Merit Systems Protection Board survey calculated that sexual harasssment cost the US federal government $189 million from May 1978 to May 1980. The figure comprises:

- replacing employees who left their jobs because of sexual harassment (to cover recruitment and training);
- paying medical insurance claims for service to employees who sought professional help because of physical or emotional stress brought on by their experiences;
- paying sick pay to employees who missed work;
- absorbing the costs caused by reductions in both individual and group productivity as a result of the disruption to work.

A minority of women acquiesce to the demands of the harasser or **fear that rejection will provoke retaliation**, particularly when the harasser is a supervisor or employer. Of women respondents to the US Merit Systems Protection Board survey, 41 per cent considered that rejection of a supervisor would lead to a worsening of working conditions, 39 per cent felt it would affect their chances of promotion or gaining a satisfactory reference, 25 per cent considered other workers would be unpleasant, and 6 per cent were afraid of losing their job. Other surveys and personal testimonies support these fears:

■ **Example:** As long as I kept saying no, my boss kept my bonuses down. I finally started dating him. I was pressured into having an affair with a 49-year-old married man. During the times I was dating my boss, my bonuses would go sky high when I refused to see him, my pay would go so low I could not pay my bills. (Clarke, 1980, p. 6.)

Retaliation takes many forms, depending on the work situation:

- verbal abuse;
- non-co-operation from male co-workers;
- poor personal recommendation/references;
- poor job evaluation/bonus rating;
- impossible performance standards;
- refusal to offer overtime;
- demotion or downgrading;
- transfer to less satisfactory work;
- worsening of shift pattern/hours worked;
- termination of employment.

The possibility of retaliation is one reason why **few women lodge a formal complaint** about harassment either with their employer or union. Other reasons include an unwillingness to make a fuss, unfamiliarity with the appropriate procedures, fear that the complaint will not be treated seriously, and the likelihood that in any case no action will be taken against the harasser. Complaints are often dealt with by personnel whose own sexist practices encourage harassment.

■ **Example:** Men in my company are not penalised for sexual encounters with co-workers, whereas women are. You feel helpless trying to confront silent accusations and using the company complaints channels when the men you talk to share a common, somewhat negative philosophy about women. (Collins and Blodgett, p. 82.)

Even if harassment is proved, managements are reluctant to discipline or dismiss supervisors or male workers. Their skills are seen as more valuable; it is the victim who is expected to adapt.

■ **Example:** My supervisor was found to have sexually harassed – but the end result was that I was literally forced by my supervisor and management to transfer to another installation. This action I took against my supervisor cost me psychologically as well as prevented promotion. (US Merit Systems Protection Board, p. 71.)

Fear that complaining may result in loss of job is well founded. Knowing that dismissal or other forms of retaliatory action are a real possibility, it is not surprising that most victims try silently to cope with harassment, irrespective of the cost to their health and future job prospects. This situation needs to be changed so that harassment is tackled openly and effectively by both management and workers. A workplace policy is vital to protect women from the consequences of harassment because, as this section highlights:

- harassment tends to get worse if it is not dealt with as quickly as possible;
- harassment is a major contributor to stress at work;
- responding to harassment by absenteeism, job-changing and quitting reinforces the view that women are unreliable workers;
- the long-term job prospects of women are damaged by transferring and changing jobs because of harassment;
- some women feel compelled to accept harassment against their will for fear of retaliation;
- without safeguards and procedures, filing a complaint can lead to retaliation, including loss of job.

## Explaining sexual harassment at work

Sexual harassment at work, in almost all cases, involves men as harassers and women as victims. It cannot be explained away as the sudden aberration of particular men with psychological problems or strange perversions. **Behaviour at work is, in fact, similar to that elsewhere.** Women are frequently whistled and shouted at in the street, manhandled in buses and trains, chatted up in pubs, and sexually abused in their own homes. Clearly the causes of this behaviour are deeply rooted in our society, and have less to do with sexual attraction than with the unequal power relationship which has existed for thousands of years between women and men.

Within the workplace this unequal power relationship is very well defined. Not only are there few women managers, employers and supervisors, but most women are employed in low-wage and low-status jobs, have little opportunity for training and promotion and are forced to work hours adapted to their other job as housewives and mothers. Sexual harassment is one way in which women are constantly reminded of their 'inferior' position in the workplace, and which prevents them from being treated as workers on the same terms as men. While not all men consciously harass women at work, **many collude with it** either by supporting the actions of others or at least by not actively doing anything to stop it. As one American male manager commented about introducing the US Equal Employment Opportunities Commission guidelines on sexual harassment to his workplace: 'These guidelines will be hard to implement because of 41,000 years of habit.' (Collins and Blodgett, p. 91.)

There are some exceptions to this general pattern. There are occasional reports of women sexually harassing men, and of men harassing other men. It is rare, however, to find women harassing other women. Because all these exceptions form such a small proportion of the total, they do not negate the general trend. In fact they may simply reflect the degree to which male patterns of predatory behaviour are accepted as so normal and natural that a few women feel it worthwhile to copy.

There are a minority of women who positively encourage sexist behaviour from male co-workers and employers, and use their sexuality to get on at work. Often it is because they have found this the only form of behaviour which brings them encouragement or reward in the job. But since it reinforces their position as a 'woman' within the workplace, playing this particular game does little to enhance long-term employment opportunities. Many women in this situation are aware of this dilemma.

■ **Example:** It tends to be the awkward men who I can get through to. I use my femininity here as a manipulative ploy and I think it is a legitimate source of attack. I find it frustrating though, as once you tend to see them that way, it tends to weaken your own position too. (Cooper and Davidson, p. 105.)

Since sexual harassment at work arises from the unequal relationship between women and men in our society, some readers might argue that little will be achieved by trying to tackle the issue at work. But it must be stressed that **such action is an essential part of the wider campaign against sexist behaviour and practices**, and subsequent sections of this handbook outline practical steps which can be taken in the workplace. It is important to recognise that:

- since women and men spend a large proportion of their lives at work, what happens there has a significant influence on their ideas and attitudes;
- unsatisfactory and unsafe working conditions, which include sexual harassment, are legitimate issues for workplace action;
- improving the status of women in the workplace by tackling sexual harassment will help increase support from all workers for improvement in the wages and job prospects of women workers.

## Summary

In this chapter, sexual harassment is revealed as a major problem for women workers. To date, such unwanted sexual comments and advances have been taken for granted in the workplace, regarded as so much a part of normal working life that few people, apart from the victim, are aware of it happening. For fear of not being believed or even laughed at, women who experience harassment feel unable to complain, preferring to cope with the stress and humiliation alone, or to leave the job.

By doing nothing to bring the issue into the open, managements, trade unions and individual workers are tacitly supporting workplace practices which are detrimental to women workers. The recent interest in the issue indicates that this situation is changing. This handbook illustrates some ways of tackling harassment, by organising a workplace campaign, for example, or negotiating special procedures for dealing with complaints. **Workers and trade unions urgently need to review their own policies** since in some instances both harasser and victim will be their members. By anticipating problems and starting to raise awareness among both men and women of those practices and attitudes which may be experienced as harassment, the actual likelihood of a serious incident may be diminished. At the same time, talking openly about the issue will help to give women who are harassed confidence that their co-workers and trade union will give them the same level of support as they would for any other workplace problem.

# 2.

# Women at work

Sexism at work / traditional women's work / working in a man's world / positive action.

Sexual harassment operates as a mechanism for reinforcing and perpetuating the disadvantage and discrimination women face at work. Individual women are subjected to humiliation and retaliation as a result of harassment. All women workers are negatively affected by a working environment which treats their sex as a significant element of their employment. Women are ghettoised into low-status, poorly-paid work; while the present economic system demands that someone undertakes this work, there is no automatic reason why this should be women. But since women are already identified within society as an inferior group, this division provides a convenient and acceptable way of selecting people for jobs. **This sexual segregation of workers, by weakening co-operation and organisation between people, increases the employers' control over the workplace.** Irrespective of the support women receive from male workers, they will continue to demand improved employment opportunities. But it is vital for the future development of the labour movement that the traditional antagonisms between women and men workers are overcome by challenging sexist attitudes and practices at work. Only in this way will workers increase their power to take effective action at the workplace.

Women's position at work is conditioned by two common assumptions – that a **woman's job opportunities and working conditions should be related to her sex** irrespective of the real work requirements, and that **women are inferior to men**. The interrelationship of these assumptions about women results in a working environment where women are treated differently and less favourably than men; an environment in which sexual harassment flourishes. Any campaign to secure a workplace free from the sexual abuse of women must therefore tackle not only the behaviour of individual men but the deep-seated and **institution-alised sexism** within most workplaces. This chapter examines various aspects of women's work experience in order to show how sexual harassment is rooted in everyday sexist practices at work. It includes:

- **the sex-segregated pattern of women's employment in Britain;**
- **examples of sexist attitudes and practices which affect women's job opportunities;**
- **the way sexism and sexual harassment operate as a form of control within traditional areas of women's work;**
- **the way sexism and sexual harassment act as a barrier to women entering non-traditional areas of employment;**
- **the need to tackle sexism and sexual harassment as part of any positive action programme.**

## Sexism at work

Sexism at work applies to those attitudes and patterns of behaviour by both employers and workers which result in women being treated differently from men in such a way that women are disadvantaged. So long as the work women do and how much they get paid is based on their sex and inferior status rather than their ability to do the job, male workers will feel able to treat women as sexually available beings rather than as co-workers. Until recently little has been published about women's experiences at work, itself a reflection of the low priority accorded to women. More is now known about the facts and figures of women's participation in the labour force. However, information about the day-to-day environment within which women work remains sketchy; as a result this section can do little more than outline some of the sexist practices and attitudes **embedded in the way work is organised.** These practices are based on a set of ideas about the paid work which women do, including the view that:

- women are best suited to particular types of jobs;
- women's work is generally less skilled than men's;
- wages are less important to women than to men;
- a part-time job is not proper work.

Each of these themes, illustrated below using a range of examples, gives rise to discrimination against women workers and creates the opportunity for male workers to exercise their power within the workplace, a power which may be used to sexually harass the women they work with.

## Women's work

In Britain, 9¼ million women undertake some paid employment, forming **40 per cent** of the total workforce. Contrary to popular myth, a large number of women have always worked outside the home; for the hundred years up to 1951 around 30 per cent of the workforce were women. Two-thirds of women workers are married and 45 per cent of women work part-time, the majority of those being married women. While part-time work is important for women, only 3 per cent of men work part-time.

Men are employed throughout all sectors of the economy. Women work in a narrow range of jobs, **three-quarters of which are in the service sector**. The three most important industries for women are: professional and scientific services, which in 1980 comprised 27 per cent of women's employment, covering jobs like laboratory assistants, secretaries, health workers; the distributive trades, with 16 per cent of women's employment, including shops and warehouses; and miscellaneous services, such as catering, cleaning and hairdressing, accounting for a further 15 per cent. While clerical work is mainly staffed by women working full-time, personal services are by far the most important employment for part-time workers. Not only are these industries the most significant areas of employment for women, but **women make up the majority of workers** in these industries. Manufacturing employs **less than 25 per cent** of women workers, who are concentrated in textiles, leather and clothing; electrical engineering; and food, drink and tobacco. Only the first employs more women than men.

The different pattern of men's and women's employment results in certain jobs and industries being identified as 'women's work'. This segregation is reinforced by the **hierarchical division** of jobs between women and men within any particular industry. A study into the employment of women by McIntosh for IFF Research showed that men accounted for 95 per cent of foremen and supervisors, 91 per cent of skilled manual workers and 87 per cent of employers and managers. Women, on the other hand, made up 48 per cent of semi-skilled and 45 per cent of unskilled manual workers. A NALGO survey of workers in local government showed that women comprised 99 per cent of typing and secretarial and 82 per cent of clerical grades, but only 24 per cent of higher professional grades. And a similar pattern also arises within manufacturing; Pollert's investigation of Churchman's tobacco factory in *Girls, Wives, Factory Lives* showed women made up 61 per cent of production workers, 35 per cent of supervisors, and 14 per cent of management. No women occupied the position of foreman! The persistence of this rigid sexual division of labour is in part the result of practices and attitudes which both directly and indirectly limit women's employment opportunities to a narrow range of jobs.

Women's paid work is closely linked to the domestic and sexual roles women are expected to perform in the home. Child-rearing and housekeeping not only restrict the time women have available for paid employment, but define the types of jobs which are 'women's work'. Women are seen as being 'naturally' attracted to jobs which service other people's needs. Cooks, cleaners, secretaries, nurses, primary teachers and barmaids are all extensions of the tasks women undertake in the home. **Women are expected to take primary responsibility for the home**, a view which affects the attitudes of employers to women workers. The IFF Research Ltd study examined employers' opinions as to why only a few women rise to senior positions or do skilled work: 39 per cent believed women were not career-conscious, 26 per cent felt family ties made women unable or unwilling to take responsibility, and 24 per cent felt that the attitudes and traditions of society were to blame. **Only 7 per cent** considered there was any problem about the attitudes of management and men generally towards women workers.

Yet **managers automatically and unconsciously look for different qualities in male and female workers**. An experiment (quoted by Harnett, 1978) showed that when men and women were interviewed for the same vaguely defined white-collar job, different characteristics were identified as important by the interviewer depending on the applicant's sex. Men were expected to be persuasive individuals, be able to change their minds on an issue, be capable of withstanding pressure, have exceptional motivation and to be aggressive. Women, however, had to have a pleasant voice, immaculate dress, excellent clerical skills, school certificates and an ability to express themselves well. While the criteria used to choose a male worker are based on decision-making and administrative abilities, the important **qualities for a woman refer to her appearance and personal**

**manner**, plus her abilities to do routine office work. In developing proposals for positive action in the workplace to improve jobs for women, the Equal Opportunities Commission list 11 negative assumptions which managements may well hold about women, which at present result in their job opportunities being restricted to traditional areas of employment:

- women lack commitment to their work;
- women's outside commitments interfere with their work;
- women possess poor mental/physical abilities for the job;
- the presence of women would produce an unfavourable reaction from other staff and/or the public;
- women are not able to supervise others;
- women are not suitable for the job because it is not a traditional area of women's work;
- women have limited career intentions;
- women are unwilling to undertake training;
- women do not conduct themselves in a businesslike way;
- women's ability to do the job is impaired by their feminine interests and experiences.

Attitudes such as these present a view of women as having special qualities because of their sex which fit them only for certain types of work; as a result it is hardly surprising that women can only get jobs in areas where they already have proven ability – those related to their role and function in the home.

## Protective legislation

Women have not chosen to be ghettoised into a limited number of jobs. Before the mid-nineteenth century, women worked in fields, factories and pits; in the two world wars women were employed in ship-building, munitions, engineering, as lorry drivers and farm labourers. Whenever the need for additional skilled labour has arisen, women have been encouraged into these areas of employment. During periods of labour surplus and unemployment, such as the 1860s and 1930s, government policies, supported by better-organised male workers who wanted to protect their own jobs and wages, closed many occupations to women. While many women were glad to leave appalling working conditions, these restrictions aroused some protest. In Lancashire the Pit Brow Lassies, working above ground in the pits, fought a long campaign to maintain their jobs, recognising that the alternative to dirty and dangerous work was either unemployment or low-wage jobs which would force them into financial dependence on their husbands.

The exodus of women from heavy industry has been accompanied by propaganda extolling the unfeminine nature of such work and promoting the vital role that women at home play in bringing up the next generation. In the nineteenth century this propaganda took the form of **protective legislation**, making the employment of women and children in the pits illegal and limiting working hours in manufacturing industry to the daytime. Whatever the current merits or otherwise of keeping this legislation, its passing presented a two-fold view of women which still influences attitudes. First, it portrayed women as in need of **protection for their own good**, to be achieved by removing them from working conditions thought too dangerous, rather than tackling those conditions. Second, it gave legal backing to the idea that **women should not take jobs from men**. Because the legislation applied only to manufacturing industry, it effectively restricted women from competing with men for the better-paid, more skilled jobs; there was no similar concern about the hours and conditions in low-paid, semi-skilled women's employment, such as dressmaking and domestic service. Today women work nights in hospitals and at cleaning offices, but without a special government order lifting the night ban, they are unable to do so in an engineering or food processing plant.

## Job titles

In some areas of work, women do undertake basically the same jobs as men, but often the jobs are described and treated differently. Common examples are male chef/female cook, salesman/shop assistant, personal assistant/secretary. **Different job titles frequently denote a status difference**, irrespective of the actual job content. This is reflected in a pay difference between men and women, on the assumption that if a man undertakes the work it must automatically involve greater responsibilities and skill. In some cases, job titles are sex-specific – workman, gasman, fisherman, postman, policeman, craftsman. While the suffix 'woman' has recently been attached to some of these titles, 'seawoman' or 'firewoman' have yet to enter common vocabulary! While the point may appear trivial, **everyday language plays a powerful role by associating particular jobs with a person's sex**. Predictably enough, housewives, hospital sisters, charwomen and tea-ladies are not jobs men seek to do.

## Skills

Women not only undertake different jobs to men but also the work they do is regarded as inferior and paid accordingly. While men monopolise higher-paid skilled and semi-skilled jobs, womens's work is often rated unskilled. Although these differences can be partly accounted for by variations in job content, there is considerable evidence to suggest that the **skill-rating of a job is closely related to the sex of the worker**.

- **Example:** Paper boxes are produced by women working on hand-fed platen machines, work which is considered and paid as unskilled labour. Cartons are produced by a more automated process requiring less individual concentration, but is rated as semi-skilled work. The carton industry employs women and men on similar jobs. Paper box production only involves women workers. Researchers found it hard not to conclude that carton production was considered semi-skilled because men are recognised as semi-skilled workers, whereas however much paper box production might qualify for upgrading, it remained unskilled because it was done by typically unskilled workers – women. (Phillips and Taylor, p. 84.)

Skills arise from the expertise a worker brings to the job and traditionally are based on long years of training. Because in the past skilled male workers could not be replaced cheaply and easily, they obtained considerable control over the job. Employers have constantly attempted to undermine this power by introducing new machinery to simplify the job and by subdividing the job into repetitive and mechanical tasks. Despite this de-skilling, the organised power of workers in these industries has enabled the majority of men's jobs to remain skilled, even though the job content and expertise involved may be reduced. What counts as skilled work today, therefore, has as much to do with the power workers can exercise to resist changes as with the actual requirement of the job. One aspect of the resistance to de-skilling was the refusal to open up jobs like printing to women for fear that their presence would automatically downgrade the work. Where women have eventually gained access to these jobs, such as in carton manufacturing, they are paid the skilled rate. But women undertaking work of similar skill in a non-male occupation receive less favourable grading.

Skills therefore depend as much on who you are as on what you do. Women's skills are undervalued because they are women and because **the skills involved in 'women's work' are treated as 'natural'**, not learnt. Women cable formers in an electronics factory were described as particularly suited to the work because it was like knitting! In *Women at Work*, Aldred compares the skills of a carpenter and a home-help. Both must be able to use hand and power tools (saws and drills/vacuum cleaner and polisher), know the correct use of chemicals (glues and varnishes/bleaches and oven cleaners), and be able to identify and carry out the necessary operations from a set of general instructions. One is paid as skilled, the other as unskilled work. The skills in traditional women's work, learnt at home over many years, are not valued because they are associated with unpaid domestic work.

In recent years, employers have attempted to both alter and compare skill levels between jobs through job evaluation and grading schemes. Their purpose has little to do with improving the skill-rating of women's work, but is rather designed to undermine traditional craft status and encourage flexibility in men's jobs. But unconscious attitudes towards the different status of women's and men's skills has resulted in **sex-biased schemes**, because the so-called scientific criteria selected for evaluation are often weighted towards men's work. The Equal Opportunities Commission booklet *Sex Bias in Job Evaluation Schemes* compares two ways of evaluating the jobs of a maintenance fitter and a company nurse. In the first, the criteria chosen for the evaluation emphasise strength, stamina, lifting and working conditions, with the result that the fitter (a man's job) is given a higher weighting because a number of similar factors, all associated with 'men's work', are used. By changing the evaluation criteria to include basic knowledge, complexity of the task, responsibility for people and mental effort, a similar evaluation is arrived at for both fitter and nurse.

In the majority of workplaces women find themselves in the lower-grade jobs:

■ **Example:** At Churchman's tobacco factory, of the eight grades, the majority of women were classed in the lowest four groups, 75 per cent were in the bottom three. Hand-stemming, done by women, was rated bottom, Grade A, whereas security patrol, a man's job, was rated Grade D. One job might hold more responsibility or danger but the other involves more physical discomfort.

A weigher's job (female) was allocated eight points for 'job knowledge and skill requirement', 8 points for 'correct practice', and 16 points for 'mental requirement'. But a zero rating for working conditions took no account of noise or tobacco dust: stiff neck, shoulders and arms were discounted under 'physical demands'. The rating committee had to decide not only what is skilled and what is not, what is comfortable and what is not, but to attach numbers to these qualities. The scheme simply reinforced job segregation by sex. (Pollert, pp. 65–77.)

Women are employed in repetitive and monotonous work, commended for their dedication and dexterity. Not only is such work unpleasant and unsatisfying but also the very qualities which women are expected to bring to the job, and which it is argued men do not have, are systematically downgraded or disregarded.

## Wages

Women's wages reflect the low status of women's jobs. Despite some progress following the Equal Pay Act 1971 towards closing the gap between men's and women's wages, **full-time women workers still earn considerably less than men**. If anything, the recent trend is towards increasing differentials between the sexes. While women earned 74 per cent of men's average hourly rate in 1977, by 1982 this had dropped to 72 per cent. There are variations between industries. In 1982 women manual workers in public administration earned 79 per cent of the male average weekly wage; women working in public services, however, received only 54 per cent of the male average weekly wage for that industry. At 68 per cent, electrical engineering has a smaller sex differential than textiles, where women earned only 62 per cent of male wages. But regardless of these differences, the overwhelming majority of women continue to be paid less than men.

Besides the differences in the basic rate between men's and women's jobs, there are a number of other **structural factors** resulting in women comprising the majority of the low paid. Basic rates are improved by a variety of measures – productivity and bonus schemes, overtime, shift premiums, and seniority pay. Far fewer women qualify for these because of the work they do and their commitments in the home. Many non-manufacturing jobs, where women provide a service, cannot easily accommodate a bonus scheme; imagine trying to measure the number of bedpans emptied by a nursing auxiliary in the course of a day. Many women cannot take on overtime because they are needed at home to prepare meals and put children to bed. Within the manufacturing sector, the opportunity for women to take shift work is limited by law. And although most women will complete 20–30 years of paid employment, the breaks in continuity caused by child-bearing and domestic responsibilities may disqualify them for seniority pay.

Low pay is also a characteristic of part-time employment. Not only are part-time workers employed for fewer hours, but part-time rates may be lower than those of full-time workers. A number of claims for equal hourly rates between part-time women and full-time men doing the same job have failed on technicalities in the Equal Pay Act. What this and the previous points illustrate is that **the current structure of wages and wage-bargaining is more closely geared to the working experiences of men** than to those of women workers.

Women's wages are a measure of the low status and skills associated with their work. At the same time, low wages are seen as justified on the grounds that **women have no need of financial independence**, a view first popularised in the last century. While in the early period of industrialisation women earned their own keep, by the second half of the nineteenth century both middle-class reformers and working-class men had pressurised women into giving up full-time work and taking responsibility for the home. Preventing women and children competing for jobs enabled men to demand higher wages to keep their families. Women serviced the family in exchange for support from the man's wage. Both male workers and employers benefited from women's unpaid labour in the home, since cleaning, cooking and child-care ensured the fitness of both current and future workers.

In fact many women continued to work; the 1911 census recorded less than 50 per cent of working-class families as being totally dependent on male wages. Women's earnings averaged around 30 per cent of family income. Nevertheless, **the ideal of the male breadwinner**, earning a family wage to cover the costs of wife and children, enabled employers to pay women minimal rates. Little has changed. Two government reports, separated by 50 years, illustrate the continuing view that women should live on their husband's income, thereby not needing higher wages.

A fair wage for a man is reckoned with reference to one who has a family of normal size; as regards women, the normal case is not that of the women with several dependants. (HM Government, 1919.)

It is necessary to consider the position of men and women separately; otherwise the problem of low pay could be practically synonymous with that of low pay among women and this could ignore the social significance of the fact that men's earnings are normally the main souce of family income. (National Prices and Incomes Board, 1971.)

Support for the male breadwinner has come not only from governments. The male-orientated trade-union movement saw in the family wage powerful arguments to increase their members' wages. Resolutions to the TUC and Labour Party in 1909, prohibiting married women from taking or keeping paid employment, were lost only after fierce debate. During the 1930s, opposition to the introduction of family allowances (now child benefit) concentrated on the likelihood of state payments undermining male bargaining power; little consideration was given to any improvements they offered to the financial position of women. Today, formal collective bargaining has moved away from family wage arguments and trade unions nationally are committed to equal pay for women. But as the figures mentioned previously show, there has been little real improvement in the differential between women's and men's wages. In the workplace, negative attitudes to women's waged work persist; women are seen as working only for something to do and to pay for the luxuries. In the following extract a chargehand and a shop steward are talking.

■ **Example:** Some women have to work. But 90 per cent it's pin money. They don't have to work, they just say 'I'll miss the company'. All that tommy rot.
You tell me – if you're an employer and you pay exactly the same to a man and a woman – which will you choose? Well, it's obvious isn't it – a man. (Pollert, pp. 79–80.)

Such views ignore the large number of women who are sole providers for their families, or the four-fold increase in poverty which would result if women were unable to work. But these attitudes, coming from trade unionists, do enable the employer to downgrade women's jobs without fear of opposition and to find methods of circumventing the Equal Pay Act by ensuring that women and men are employed in different jobs.

## Part-time work

Of all women workers, 45 per cent work less than 30 hours a week; the majority of part-time workers are women. Part-time work is typical of retailing, personal services and many women's jobs in the public sector. While a minority work short hours by choice, for most women paid work must be fitted in around domestic responsibilities. Given the lack of nurseries, women with young children find daytime work difficult, often seeking employment on twilight shifts when their husbands are at home. Once children are at school, finishing times and school holidays limit the opportunities to work a full 35–40 hour week. Women working part-time suffer double discrimination: as well as being subjected to all the disadvantages experienced by full-time women workers, **less favourable rights and opportunities are attached to part-time** as compared to full-time work. Legal employment rights, pay structures and working practices are geared to the male worker's employment pattern – eight hours a day, five days a week for 40 years or more. Little account has been taken of the normal work pattern for women – up to 10 years of full-time work, a period out of employment, a return to part-time work and perhaps finally another period of full-time employment.

Statutory employment rights depend on a worker being employed for 16 or more hours a week. By working less hours, **120,000 women lost some legal protection** in 1981; more than half this number had no protection at all. The statutory rights dependent on 16+ hours worked a week (or 8+ hours for five years or more, employment at one workplace) are:

- unfair dismissal;
- unfair dimissal for pregnancy;
- written reason for dismissal;
- minimum period of notice;
- written statement of contract terms and conditions;
- maternity pay;
- reinstatement after childbirth;
- redundancy pay;
- time off to look for work;
- written statement of redundancy pay calculation;

- guarantee pay;
- medical suspension pay;
- itemised pay statement.

As regards pay, according to a Low Pay Unit survey, 74 per cent of part-time workers earn less than two-thirds of the average male wage. Women part-time workers also earn 20 per cent less per hour than full-time women workers, not only because they work in some of the lowest-paid occupations, but because **employers often pay lower rates to part-timers** doing the same job as a full-time worker. In one instance, a secretary at the National Union of Agricultural and Allied Workers found she was paid a lower hourly rate than full-time secretaries. Her claim for equal pay failed at the tribunal because the full-time workers were women, not men.

Many part-time workers claiming equal pay have found their applications refused. In two cases, part-time women machinists in the clothing industry who claimed equal hourly rates with full-time men machinists lost their case on the grounds that their jobs were materially different. The Employment Appeal Tribunal ruled that while the men's machines were operated for a full day, the women's machines were idle for some hours, costing the employer money. Although both men and women produced the same when they were at work, and the employer could have taken on other part-time workers to cover the idle hours, the lower hourly rate was ruled as justified because the work was part-time. By undermining the value of part-time work, the tribunal reinforced discriminatory attitudes towards women.

By **not treating part-time work as a normal pattern of employment**, women workers lose many of the benefits negotiated for full-time workers. Full-time employee status is a usual qualification for holiday pay, employers' pension schemes, shift and overtime pay. While part-time workers earning more than £32.50 a week benefit from the new Statutory Sick Pay, only one-third of part-time women workers are covered by employers' sick schemes, compared with 80 per cent of full-time women workers. Few part-timers have access to training or promotion; irrespective of experience or length of service, women working part-time are expected to stay in the lowest grades. All these practices discriminate against women workers. One recent tribunal judgment recognised this. Part-time women workers at Eley Kynock in Birmingham filed a complaint against their employer's redundancy agreement because it protected full-time workers by laying off part-timers first. They successfully argued that since the full-time workers were men and the part-timers women, women were being treated worse. They won the case, but as yet it remains one of the few positive actions in support of part-time women.

## Summary

As these examples show, working life is deeply imbued with sexist attitudes and practices. Sexism goes beyond the casual shop floor remark or unsympathetic manager to encompass the **structures and organisation of work**. Job segregation, job titles, protective legislation, skill designation and job evaluation, the family wage and attitudes to part-time workers illustrate the degree to which women's opportunities at work are defined by their sex and inferior status. By denying women fair treatment and respect at work, institutionalised sexism provides an environment in which sexual harassment flourishes.

# Traditional women's work

Women's paid employment reflects the roles and tasks women traditionally undertake in the home. Not only is this work characterised by the utilisation of domestic skills, but as at home, women perform a range of services for men. The qualities associated with being a woman – physical attractiveness, caring for others, willingness to please, passivity and compliance – with their suggestions of sexual availability, have become integrated into the **occupational requirements** of many traditional jobs. Women employed because their sex is considered an essential aspect of the job are inevitably vulnerable to sexual exploitation. Sexist behaviour and harassment by men in the workplace is a constant reminder that their job may be more dependent on their attractiveness than their skills, thus undermining confidence in their ability to get alternative employment. By exercising power in this way, **men reinforce and maintain their authority and control** in the workplace.

This link between sexual harassment and the sexual assumptions in-built in women's work can be illustrated by looking at three main occupational areas – secretarial work, personal services and the feminine professions. Each type of job exploits aspects of femininity; while sexual harassment is prevalent in all, the particular characteristics of each job influencing the actual pattern of harassment.

## The office 'wife'

Secretarial work has traditionally been marketed as a safe job for women; a pleasant and clean working environment, skills always in demand, opportunities to return to part-time work, maybe the chance of promotion into lower management. Although the advent of new technology is challenging this image, the reality has never been quite this rosy. Secretaries are not paid as skilled workers, despite training in shorthand, typing, book-keeping and office administration. While technical skills are undervalued, a good secretary is expected to look after her boss. **Secretaries act as office wives** – keeping the place tidy, serving drinks, fetching and carrying, answering the phone, smoothing over disappointments. Secretarial attributes most sought after by managers include the ability to anticipate and take care of personal needs and a deferential manner towards men.

A feminine appearance is important; a decorative secretary will be the envy of colleagues, a hint of sexiness may be enough to clinch a difficult business deal. Many secretaries recognise the implicit way in which sex is part of their job. Their experience is summarised by Benet (1972):

> The first thing that comes to many a man's mind when he thinks about secretaries is sex . . . Men in offices speculate endlessly about the girls, comparing them, picking favourites, teasing them. In fact, most office men will tell you that's why the girls are there. The sexual roles that women play in real life have been transferred to the office.

In this environment, sexual harassment is an occupational hazard. The comedian's patter about 'having it off with the secretary' trivialises a serious problem. Because the working relationship between boss and secretary is based on serving his needs, women find it difficult to avoid sexual advances. Being alone together in the office, accepting a lunch invitation and working late are all part of the job.

**Example:** Adrienne Tomkins, a secretary, was invited to lunch by her boss, ostensibly to discuss his recommendation for her promotion. At the bar, her boss began drinking heavily. When it became apparent that work was not going to be discussed, she asked to return to work. By threats of retaliation against her as an employee, threats of physical force and finally exercise of physical restraint, her boss kept her at the bar against her will for several hours. He expressed a desire to have sexual relations with her, saying it was necessary to their satisfactory working relationship. When she tried to leave he physically prevented her, implying that if she protested no one at the company would help her. Fearing for her job and physical safety, she remained. Her boss grabbed her and kissed her on the mouth. (McKinnon, p. 71.)

Although personal secretaries comprise the minority of female office workers, the image of the boss/secretary relationship extends to all levels of office life. Over 90 per cent of clerical workers are women, the majority work for men. Clerks, typists, switchboard operators are subjected to the same treatment.

■ **Example:** In our main open plan office there are about 20 women and a few men. Some of us were warned before we joined and we always try to warn a new woman on her first day about the office groper, that's what we call the supervisor. He's about 34, married, and his office is just along the corridor from where we all sit. He shares it with his secretary. She's 25 and married. She keeps a little bell on her desk and when his physical advances get too difficult for her to handle, she rings it. He does it to us all because the coffee machine is just outside his door and when you go to it, you have to take a ruler with you because as you bend down to get your drink he jumps out from behind his door and grabs you. He holds you round the waist and then moves his hands upwards and tries to get hold of your breasts. (Read, p. 60.)

### Serving the public

Secretaries are not the only workers who find their sexuality an important part of the job. An attractive appearance, a sympathetic ear, and just a hint of hidden sexual pleasure are major qualifications for a range of occupations in the service sector. Implicit sexual availability of female staff sells holidays, airline tickets, hotel accommodation, food and drink, savings accounts, entertainment and manufactured goods to a large number of male customers. Receptionists and air hostesses are expected to be demurely inviting, offering in the words of the advert that 'special kind of person-to-person service'. For waitresses and barmaids, overt suggestions of sexual interest are part of the job description. A barmaid who refuses to flirt with customers risks dismissal; a night-club waitress who questions her revealing costume will be labelled unsuitable. Their jobs involve working unsocial hours, dealing efficiently with customer orders and coping with tired and aching feet, all for very low wages. In addition, **working conditions include sexual harassment by customers** as well as employers and co-workers. Pleasing the customer is absolutely essential when wages have to be topped up from tips.

- **Example:** Men think they have the right to touch me and proposition me because I am a waitress. Why do women have to put up with this sort of thing anyway? You aren't in a position to say 'get your crummy hands off me', because you need the tips. That's what a waitress job is all about. (McKinnon, p. 44.)

Because it is good for business, employers rarely support women who complain of harassment. Whether the incident occurs during a hotel lunch or at a late-night club, the customer is always right. By requiring employees to accept or even encourage harassment from customers, the employer or manager is able to make similar demands. As elsewhere, a refusal brings dismissal or a deterioration in working conditions. In occupations where women depend heavily on tips, being required to serve the wrong tables or to work a quiet shift can have dramatic effects on earnings. A woman who refuses to acquiesce to sexual harassment may find herself shunned by her co-workers since by not pleasing the customer she puts everyone's economic survival at risk. Her isolation is reinforced by a deliberately fostered rivalry between workers and the difficulties faced by trade unions in organising small workplaces.

Women working in other personal services – shop assistants, bus conductresses, cleaners, home-helps – may not sell sex as part of their job; nevertheless, while at work they too are harassed both by customers and people they work with. Because of their difficulties in obtaining better-paid jobs, this work is often done by black women, who face abuse because of their colour as well as their sex. Women working in many service jobs often finish late and have to travel home alone at night. Ever-present in this situation is the danger of attack not only from a stranger but from a customer or co-worker aware of the time a woman leaves work.

Statistical evidence shows that the majority of sexual attacks on women are by male friends and acquaintances.

## The feminine professions

Not all women's work is unskilled. Towards the end of the nineteenth century middle-class women began demanding access to professional jobs, particularly so that those who did not want to marry could pursue a secure and satisfying career. In the face of considerable male opposition, women found their way into medicine and teaching, occupations associated with essentially feminine skills. **Looking after people became professionalised.** Today, large numbers of women are nurses, teachers and social workers, jobs demanding a sensitive and responsive approach to people's needs. Women engaged in the feminine professions are responsible for the upbringing of children, the care of the sick and the elderly, and the provision of emotional support for people at times of stress. Such activities mirror those that women undertake in the home. Of the two major roles women perform in the family, as wife/mother and as sexual partner, it is the mothering role which is most closely associated with professional jobs. Nevertheless, there are pressures in these jobs for women to act as sexual beings. Nurses are one example, so often portrayed as part-angel, part-girlfriend whose task it is to re-build the self-confidence of male patients by reinforcing their masculinity through reference to their obvious, if temporarily impaired, sexual prowess and attraction. Not surprisingly, nurses experience sexual harassment from patients as well as co-workers.

Social workers and teachers too are vulnerable to harassment from clients of all ages. Adolescent boys are particularly likely to pick on a woman teacher's sexuality as a means of causing trouble and undermining her authority.

■ **Example:** New members of staff and students on teaching practice were the principal targets of sexual abuse. The general tactic employed by the boys was to 'make a grab' while milling around in a group on the stairs or in a corridor, and then run, leaving the victim unsure of the identity of the offender and frightened to make false accusations. Equally humiliating were the obscenities shouted from a distance or the appraising remarks exchanged within hearing. (Whitbread, p. 91.)

As in other workplaces, sexual harassment remains a hidden issue in most schools. Sexist attitudes and behaviour are reflected in formal teaching and through personal relationships both of staff and pupils. Training to be a professional worker involves a minimum of 16 years in the education system. Sexual harassment starts in the playground; girls are pestered and verbally abused from an early age by their male contemporaries. In the safety of the staff-room, male teachers comment on the sexual characteristics of their female pupils. As students in higher education, women become subject to the same pressures for sexual favours from their male lecturers and tutors as women workers experience from a supervisor. Tutors are powerful because they are responsible for both the personal welfare of students and the control of examination marks. A failed degree is as serious as dismissal from work.

## Working in a man's world

Not all women work in jobs which are closely related to their sexual identity. For the minority of women who work in manufacturing industry, the link between employment and their sex is indirect. Sex and femininity are not marketed as part of the job; however, being a woman ensures the work is low-status and low-paid. Skilled workers in manufacturing are mostly men, as are foremen and managers. The examples of sexism given earlier demonstrate how the attitudes of male workers act as a barrier to the revaluation of women's skills and limit their access to new areas of work. Nevertheless, increasing numbers of women are seeking employment in non-traditional areas of work in the manual craft trades and in managerial and professional jobs. In entering these fields, women have to tackle prejudices about their unsuitability for such 'unfeminine' work, and overt hostility from male workers afraid of losing control over working practices. Where this control operates in declining industries, like printing and engineering, genuine fears about de-skilling and job losses mask discriminatory attitudes towards women. The problem of long-term unemployment cannot be solved by keeping women out of skilled jobs. On the contrary, recovery depends on an economic development programme which is unlikely to gain widespread support if it denies employment opportunities to women.

Discriminatory practices include sexual harassment. The distress and humiliation resulting from unwanted sexual remarks and behaviour operates as a mechanism of control. Women are reminded that managers, foremen and skilled male workers hold the power in the workplace and that access to new jobs depends on their agreement. **Harassment is a way of warning interlopers that they do not belong.** The experiences of women working in factories, those in management and the professions and of women entering manual trades illustrate the degree to which harassment and sexist attitudes limit women's employment opportunities.

## Factory 'girls'

Manufacturing industry employs women in food, drink and tobacco processing, textiles and clothing, and electrical engineering. Within the factory women work at the less skilled, monotonous jobs, ruled by the conveyor belt and the stop watch. Few men work alongside women; apart from the foreman these sections of the workplace are wholly dependent on female labour. Men work elsewhere, in maintenance, stores, the warehouse. Unlike working environments which foster competition between women, the shop floor engenders solidarity and sisterly support. Everyone's job is the same, opportunities for advancement are non-existent. Chatting about family problems or a favourite television programme helps cope with stress and boredom. The few men who may work in the section appear outsiders, unable or unwilling to participate in such a female world. Anyone walking round the workplace might assume that women working there are free from the sexist attitudes and abuse found elsewhere.

This apparent dominance of women on the shop floor masks the control men have over factory life. Calling women 'girls' is one reminder of their real status as workers; girls, being less than adult, cannot expect responsibility or higher wages. Whistling and catcalls greet women who leave their own section; pin-ups and soft-porn calendars paper the foreman's office. In such an atmosphere, women are offered few ways of relating to male workers and supervisors except by playing on their sexuality; by doing so they unintentionally reinforce their inferior position in the workplace. In *Girls, Wives, Factory Lives*, Pollert explores how sexism and harassment are used against women; the extract quoted here gives a useful insight into shop-floor life.

Not only were they subjected to the discipline of work and of factory rules, on top of this, as women they were exposed to constant sexist patronisation, not just from chargehands and foremen, but from any men that worked around them: 'Hey gorgeous', 'Do us a favour, luv', 'Come here, sexy' – all are familiar addresses for women. Supervision was sexually oppressive and the manner usually cajoling, laced with intimate innuendo, and provocative jokes, hands placed on girls' shoulders as they worked, imposition mixed with flattery. To survive with some pride, without melting into blushes or falling through the floor, the girls had to keep on their toes, have a ready answer, fight back. They were forced into a defensive-aggressive strategy – but always on the men's terms. They had to collude. And in this they also colluded with the language of control.

The use of female sex appeal as a way of getting round their supervisor, or retaliating against authority was always a double-edged weapon, which in the long term hurt them and nobody else. For if they won momentary victories of self-assertion, it was only by colluding with the conventional male attitudes towards the female as sex-object, and laid them open to sexist advances whether they liked it or not.

Because there were some [women] who would not or could not join the repartee and fit the parts of both worker and sex-object, they were more prone to arbitrary victimisation, not only for breaches in disciplinary rules, but also for failing the PPS [proficiency payments scheme] standards. They failed to 'please'.

Despite being disguised as a joke, assumptions about the sexual availability of women still results in stress and humiliation. The banter hides, but does not remove, the power which men have over women at work.

■ **Example:** There is an engineer who puts his hands all over the place and sort of pushes himself against you. It's really creepy. I sit down when I see him coming so as he can't get to me. I was sitting at the conveyor belt one day when one of the blokes came up to me and rubbed his chisel on my breasts. It made me so angry that I grabbed it off him and threw it.

There is one man who has a problem, he stares at me. I've told him to piss off but he just laughs. I've tried ignoring him but it seemed at one time wherever I went in the factory he was always there. Now I only see him at meal times in the canteen. It got really bad. I'd got to the stage when I used to hate going up there for my dinner, it really upset me. I couldn't go and complain, they might get you on the way home. I don't want to risk that. Anyway, they'd say he hadn't done much, wouldn't they? (Read, p. 39.)

Rather than make a complaint which may well not be taken seriously, women learn to cope with unwanted advances. But telling a co-worker to 'piss off' offers only temporary respite and masks the stress of waiting for the next time. Occasionally a whole section of workers may become sufficiently angry to take action against the harasser – if perhaps a woman is being constantly victimised. A group of women may hassle the foreman in the lift or shout abuse so that the whole factory can hear. Effective as this may be in the short term by embarrassing the offender, it does little to challenge the sexist culture of the workplace. In consequence, women remain an inferior section of the workforce, because both management and male workers continue to see them as women first and not workers.

### Entering management and the professions

Less than 20 per cent of managers in Britain are women. Of these, the majority work in shops, offices and catering, areas where their staff are mainly women. Few are employed as production or works managers, in transport or on sites. However, an increasing number of women are entering management and the professions – as administrators and supervisors, in sales and stock control, as architects, lawyers and engineers. Breaking into a man's world is not easy. Much of the work in management depends on the contacts and mutual trust built up through 'the old boy network'. Women are outsiders. Male exclusiveness cuts women off from vital business activities. Women managers report instances of being left out of weekly lunches at the club, the important session on the golf course, the after-hours drink. **Women challenge this cosy world**, for these are the same men who chat up barmaids and harass secretaries. Keeping women out can go as far as subtle sabotage of career prospects. In one case, a barrister, the first woman in a particular set of chambers, realised she was being given all the awkward cases to deal with in the hope that eventually she would become dissatisfied and leave. Skills may be undervalued, with colleagues treating a woman as a glorified secretary who is incapable of coping with more complex aspects of the job. To prove themselves, women feel the need to work harder and take on difficult assignments. The pressure they are under is increased by the knowledge that failure will not only affect their own job prospects but may make it difficult for other women to obtain employment in the future.

In this atmosphere of subtle hostility women can find it difficult to maintain their individuality. By adopting the personal manner and style of work which men identify with their sex, women in managerial and professional jobs can find it easier to get along with male colleagues. But projecting their femininity above work skills carries the danger that their abilities will not be recognised. Nevertheless, Cooper and Davidson discovered that 77 per cent of women managers they surveyed felt it necessary **to assume a sex-stereotyped role**. The most common image presented by women emphasises their mothering role; as confidante and counsellor women find themselves supporting their male colleagues in times of stress. In consequence they may become so busy helping others, their own career needs remain secondary, a situation similar to that which women also face outside work. Other women find it easier to project an image of themselves as sex-object, or find such a role assigned to them by colleagues whether they like it or not. However, being labelled a seductress can result in their work not being taken seriously; male co-workers may shy away from working with them for fear of gossip. At the same time, they can be treated as the office mascot, the token woman, taken along to meetings for their decorative qualities rather than their skills. Some women are unable or unwilling to play either of these roles, preferring to suppress any hint of femininity behind a hard, authoritarian exterior. In fact, far from disassociating themselves from commonly identified female roles, such women find themselves stereotyped as 'man-haters' or 'iron maidens', women that men consider difficult to work with. Women managers who adopt this approach end up isolated even though their competence at the job may well be recognised.

Although women in management and the professions may appear to have successfully entered a man's world, their position within it is precarious. Despite their jobs, their identity as women continues to condition their treatment at work. High status does not eliminate sexual harassment.

■ **Example:** I have a terrible relationship with my boss. We have tried to talk about it but he finds it difficult to relate to women. I try to cope by keeping a low profile but that causes problems in my work performance and communication. He sees me as a sexual being and there is constant sexual harassment. There was a woman in the job before me and she suffered the same and left because of it. I may have to leave the job as well. (Cooper and Davidson, p. 104.)

Harassment is not just a hazard at work; frequently women have indicated that the only way they can survive a business trip or conference is to shut themselves away in their hotel room to avoid the unwanted attentions of men. Women travelling alone are automatically assumed to be sexually available. Harassment, as one aspect of the sexism women experience working in a male environment, reinforces stress and isolation. Women managers who are harassed have few women colleagues to turn to for support; the only other women are likely to be junior staff. Under such circumstances, leaving the job may seem the only option. In taking such action women perpetuate the view that they are unsuitable for jobs involving decision-making and responsibility. Male attitudes and behaviour have ensured such jobs remain a male preserve.

## Women in manual trades

Opportunities for women to work in non-traditional jobs are occurring not only in white-collar occupations but in those jobs requiring craft skills. Although still a tiny minority, young women are working as plumbers, welders, carpenters, motor vehicle mechanics, printers, telephone engineers and technicians. The traditional route for obtaining the relevant skills is to serve an apprenticeship where on-the-job training is coupled with day-release or evening study. After serving time, acquiring the appropriate qualifications offers entry into an elite group of workers whose skills have enabled them to tightly control their terms and conditions of employment. Although there have been some job losses in the current period, particularly in the building industry, union organisation remains strong relative to other areas of work. The continuing demand for craft skills has ensured that those who have lost jobs in manufacturing and the public sector can find work, perhaps by becoming self-employed. This relative job security, coupled with wage rates higher than those for other manual jobs, makes access to craft trades attractive to women seeking to break away from low-wage unskilled work. One obstacle is finding opportunities to acquire the relevant skills; in response to demand a few special courses have been set up for this purpose. Once trained, women face the second hurdle – to be taken on in a workplace sympathetic to employing women. With the exception of a few local authorities who have positively encouraged women to join their direct labour force, the hostility shown towards women who try to enter craft areas has resulted in them setting up women's workshops and co-operatives.

Negative attitudes and behaviour towards women, which includes sexual harassment, is widespread in the craft trades. Women attending training courses experience hostility from both instructors and other trainees who view their presence as an intrusion. Instructors find fault with the work women do, picking on common mistakes made by male trainees without drawing comment. At the same time instructors patronise women by setting low expectations for achievement and over-praising any task completed adequately. Both instructors and trainees are threatened by women entering their world. In one instance a woman attending an otherwise all-male painting and decorating course found her work constantly defaced with sexually explicit graffiti. She was subjected to verbal abuse about her body and clothes, and the level of intimidation increased to include being stopped on her way home and physically threatened by her co-trainees. Her instructor, although aware of the situation, took no action.

Harassment continues after women find work. Women working on building sites or in a workshop are breaking into a tightly-knit male group. All new workers are set initiation tests; for women these are often more dangerous and difficult. One woman on her own had to shift a large pile of lorry tyres across the stores; another was made to use a pneumatic drill without proper training. Complaining to a foreman or supervisor is unlikely to bring support. Women are disciplined for offences men get away with every day, like swearing at the site foreman. Sexist comments, touching, flashing, demands for sex are almost part of the job. As the only woman in the workplace, the feeling of isolation and intimidation can be overwhelming. Women's interests rarely feature in the conversation; men talk about their world – football, motorbikes, last night at the pub.

■ **Example:** There are days when no one says anything to m
except 'Can I borrow a spanner' or 'Hurry up with that car'
One of them makes really hostile jokes about women whe
I'm around. Work is really exhausting and I think it is wors
because I have no friendly support at work. It could be muc
easier if I had someone sympathetic to talk to. All the time
feel as if I'm in the middle of a jungle. (Coote, p. 76.)

Hostility towards women from men working in manual trade
arises from a complex set of attitudes. Craftsmen fear that
women, whom they have been brought up to consider as mech
anically illiterate, can do these jobs, their own status and ear
ings will decrease. This fear was clearly identified by Cockburn i
her recent study of male workers in the printing industry. In he
book *Brothers*, male workers talked about their feelings towarc
women being recruited into the trade.

■ **Example:** Some of the shine would go out of the job for me
Prestige might not be exactly the right word, but it carries wha
is known as a macho bit, composing. It's man's work. If yo
hear of a man secretary, a lot of people raise a few eyebrow
Well it's the same with a woman working alongside a ma
doing *his* job. They would say – even though a woman is doir
what has been a man's job, they would tend to think tha
because the woman is there, the man is now doing a *woman*
job. You might only have one woman working with nine mei
But if I said to my mates I was working with a woman, the
would feel, say, oh, he's doing a woman's job – because the
see a woman *can* do it. They wouldn't think to say that she
the one doing a man's job. (Cockburn, p. 180.)

As men see it, women, because of their sex, should not unde
take dirty, heavy work using dangerous tools. But the thre
posed by women goes beyond fears about work status; it attacl
deeply-held views of femininity and masculinity. Women wh
work in manual trades rarely conform to traditional stereotype
the very nature of the work makes this impossible. Wearir
baggy overalls, lifting heavy objects, using power tools, gettir
dirty and dusty, contradicts conventional images of wome
Both sexes are brought up to accept that their sexual identi
fixes their behaviour and interests. Working in manual trade
women challenge the view that they are born with specific qua
ities associated with being a woman. By shattering assumptio

that they function best as mothers and sex-objects, craftswomen create insecurity and bewilderment in men. Subconsciously there is a fear that if women are not quite what men were led to believe, then maybe **their own male identity is also in question**. Uncomfortable thoughts are more easily put to the back of the mind than sorted out, particularly when social convention makes it difficult for men to talk openly about their feelings. Suppressing such fears gives rise to overt hostility towards women co-workers aimed at undermining their self-confidence and driving them out of the job.

# Positive action

Women are discriminated against at work through the operation of institutionalised sexism. The structure of employment in Britain operates in favour of men who are not expected to combine work with domestic activities. Women's work experience is conditioned by their sex. They are disadvantaged at work because the attitudes and behaviour of employers and workers assume that women workers are both different from and inferior to men. But in recent years the inevitability of women's unsatisfactory position at work has begun to be challenged. A range of women's organisations, together with trade unions are developing programmes to improve work opportunities for women.

The aim of positive action programmes is **to identify and eliminate those workplace practices which ghettoise women into low-paid, unskilled work and to set up mechanisms designed to encourage women into non-traditional occupations**. In 1980 the TUC issued a consultative document outlining key aspects of such a programme, which can be summarised as:

- employers should publicly declare themselves equal opportunity employers;
- job evaluation schemes should not differentiate between male and female skills;
- job descriptions should not imply sex-stereotyping of jobs;
- criteria for promotion should not discriminate against women;
- recruitment policies should actively encourage women to apply for all types of jobs;
- personnel staff should be trained in equal opportunities policy;

- interviews should not include questions which discriminate against women;
- working conditions should be examined to ensure women can take up employment, by providing a creche, more flexible working hours and maternity facilities.

Other programmes include the need to analyse the current work-force in order to identify jobs where women are either under- or over-represented and the setting up of special training programmes to provide women with the skills and experience necessary to take on new areas of work. In *Positive Action for Women* (Robarts, Coote and Ball, 1981) programmes set up by ICI, Sainsbury's and Rank Xerox are examined, together with hints for both individuals and groups about how to negotiate such a programme with the employer.

Similar programmes, under the title of affirmative action, have been in operation in the USA for some years. Although the detailed provisions are different from those in Britain, because they place more reliance on legal measures than on trade-union action, the aims are the same. Experience has shown, however, that despite some progress in opening up new jobs, the majority of women continue to work in low-wage, unskilled jobs. Farley (1978) identifies sexual harassment as a key element in this lack of progress:

> Occupational equality is a major goal of Affirmative Action. Unfortunately, it has been a goal in a campaign to raise female wages and opportunities without an adequate analysis of the means by which men have traditionally controlled female labour. And so, male sexual harassment – which ensures the maintenance of job segregation – has gone largely unchallenged.

Any positive action programme in Britain is likely to come up against similar barriers to progress. Reviewing training, child-care facilities and job evaluation schemes are important, but restructuring the organisation and operation of the workplace is not enough. A **positive action programme must take into account the deeply-held sexist attitudes** which permeate all levels of working life. Sexual harassment needs to be treated as a serious workplace issue by both management and workers. Continuing to treat women first as sex-objects and playthings rather than workers, to address them as girls and praise their looks rather

han their competence, will not build the confidence women
need to apply for promotion or to train in new skills. Few are
likely to do so anyway if they know their entry into a new work
area will generate overt hostility.

Achieving equal opportunities for women means creating a
workplace free from sexual harassment and the institutionalised
sexism which enables harassment to flourish. This handbook
identifies some of the ways in which workers and trade unions
can begin to tackle sexist practices and attitudes in their own
workplace. While the chapters on individual action and the law
are aimed at women who are being harassed and who have no
trade-union support, the chapters on trade unions, workplace
campaigns and collective agreements cover wider campaigning
issues. By developing these ideas to fit individual workplaces, it
should be possible to draw up a plan of action to challenge both
harassment and the general sexist environment at work.

# Part 2:
## Taking action

# 3.

# Individual action

Avoiding harassment / getting support / keeping a written record / complaining / retaliating / contacting women's groups / assertiveness and self-defence.

All women should be able to work in a harassment-free workplace. Sexual harassment needs to be stopped before it results in a woman leaving her job or suffering retaliatory action. Removing harassment from the workplace requires action against both individual incidents and those sexist practices and attitudes at work which foster harassment.

The most effective way of taking up this challenge is through **trade-union organisation and campaigning**. However, 60 per cent of women workers are not members of trade unions, because either they are not convinced that trade unions represent their specific problems and interests, or their workplace and occupation are hard to organise. Women employed in private offices, small shops, cafes and restaurants, launderettes, hairdressers, and other services have had little contact with trade unions, which themselves find difficulty in organising small, scattered workplaces. Even under these circumstances, **joining a trade union** offers women the most effective long-term protection against persistent harassment. Information about trade unions relevant to a particular area or occupation should be available at the town hall, local advice centre or Citizens Advice Bureau, public library or the secretary of the local Trades Council.

Becoming a trade-union member is not, however, a practical step for all women and unless the union is already well organised, joining will not solve immediate problems. In workplaces which lack collective organisation, it is still possible to take some action to stop sexual harassment.

This chapter examines ways in which women have tackled the issue where they are on their own without trade-union support.

**None are ideal solutions**. In an already stressful situation, the onus is on the victim to challenge the harasser. Without support, it is easy for the victim to blame herself for the harassment and to feel guilty at causing trouble for the harasser. By standing up for herself, a woman working in a badly organised workplace risks disciplinary action. Preparing for a backlash must be part of any action taken by a victim against her harasser. Despite these problems, it is better to do something about harassment than to try and ignore it. Persistent harassment has long-term consequences for work performance and health. Immediate action following an initial incident of harassment is more likely to be effective than hoping it will stop; later, the only practical solution may seem to be leaving the job. Individual action might include:

- **taking steps to avoid harassment;**
- **seeking support from other workers;**
- **keeping a written record of incidents;**
- **making a complaint of harassment;**
- **taking retaliatory action;**
- **contacting women's groups;**
- **training in assertiveness and self-defence.**

## Avoiding harassment

The most common reaction to a complaint of sexual harassment is that a woman 'asked for it'. **While it is very unfair** that the victim rather than the harasser should have to modify her behaviour, your credibility when making a complaint may increase if you cannot easily be accused of provocation or of misleading the harasser. At the same time, taking avoiding action may reduce the number of occasions when harassment could occur.

**1.** Try to keep your relationship with the harasser on a professional level. Ensure there are **valid business reasons** for lunches and after-hours meetings, and avoid the friendly chat after work.

**2.** If you are asked to work late, try to arrange this when **other people are also working**. If you do not want to stay, make an excuse on the grounds of a previous engagement, etc.

**3.** If you have to work in the same room as the harasser, **leave the door open or arrange for a co-worker to interrupt from time to time**. In one instance (see p. 42) a woman kept a small bell on her desk and rung it whenever she needed help. Better still, find a pretext for transferring your work to a more crowded area.

**4.** Avoid asking for special treatment which may make you indebted to the harasser. **Try not to do personal favours** for him, such as buying a present or arranging a social activity, which are beyond the specific requirements of your job.

**5.** Avoid talking to the harasser about your personal life. If you are upset, he may take this as an invitation to comfort you. At the same time, politely **refuse to discuss any of his personal problems**; it is easy to be drawn into the role of counsellor and emotional prop.

**6.** Finally, think about what you wear. Although the harasser will make advances regardless of your dress, it is easier to get support from others if your clothes are considered suitable for work. **Avoid giving anyone the excuse not to take you seriously.**

## Getting support

**Talk with other women in your workplace.** Find out if they too have experienced harassment from the same man. By doing this you will feel less isolated and stop blaming yourself for the incidents. If you are not sure how to bring the subject up directly, you could start a discussion over lunch about cases you know about or use some of the information in this book. At the same time, make sure you are sympathetic to other women who say they have been harassed. Once you discover you are not alone, you may want to meet regularly as a group to talk about workplace problems and sort out ways of tackling harassment together. Realising you are not alone will bring you confidence to take further action.

If the women you work with are not sympathetic, **look for support outside work**. You could contact a women's group or organisation (see p. 66), or talk to relatives or friends. If harassment is making you ill, tell your doctor about it. Women who live with a man have different views about discussing the problem with their partner. In most cases it will help, since keeping secrets simply adds to the emotional stress. Sometimes, however, husbands or boyfriends fail to understand the seriousness of the issue; alternatively, they may threaten immediate action against the harasser. If you think either reaction is likely, ask a friend who is aware of your problem and feelings to be there when you talk about it.

## Keeping a written record

Collecting evidence of harassment will enable you to make a complaint or refute unsavoury allegations at a later date. Written evidence would also be helpful at a tribunal hearing. **Keep a diary or notebook** handy to record **each incident**; because she had nothing else handy, one woman produced her record written on matchboxes and paper serviettes. You should record:

● date of incident;
● location of incident;
● time of incident;
● nature of incident (to cover both actions and comments of the harasser);
● your response;
● your feelings at the time;
● name of any witnesses.

An entry could read as follows:

■ 2 January 1983 – corridor between finance and typing pool, 2.30 p.m.
Mr Jones stopped me, asked about progress of typing, remarked on the colour of my jumper, and stroked my arm, touching my left breast, asked me to bring typing to his office a.s.a.p., winked as he walked on.

Cowered as he touched me and started to move down the corridor, said nothing except would check the typing, felt sick and panic-stricken.

Mary Reed came through door at end of corridor, saw us together, but too far away to record details. Is willing to say that.

While collecting evidence, **prepare for any possible backlash** by also keeping a record of your own work. If possible, obtain a copy of your personal file to check there is nothing which can be used against you. Note down the jobs you are asked to do and any problems which arise in completing them. Record any comments you receive about your work, particularly when you are praised for working well. This information will be useful if the harasser tries to destroy your credibility following a complaint. Make sure you keep all this information in a safe place. One woman found out what her boss thought of her only when he left on his desk an open diary which contained his scribbled pornographic comments!

# Complaining

As soon as possible after the harassment starts, you should **make it clear you do not like this behaviour**. A simple statement will do, such as, 'Mr Jones, I do not like you touching me, so please can you stop.' This may be the first time anyone has mentioned it and it could be enough to change the harasser's behaviour. If you leave it too long it will become more difficult to find the 'right' opportunity and the harasser may feel he has more grounds for saying you enjoyed it. If the harassment continues, you will need to consider more **formal methods of complaining**. You could do this in a number of ways.

**1.** Approach the harasser for an **informal discussion**, taking a friend with you. Outline the occasions when you have been harassed, make it clear you want the harassment to stop. Say that although you would prefer to keep the matter private, you would make a formal complaint if necessary. Make sure the harasser is clear about the sort of behaviour which offends you.

**2. Write a letter** to the harasser indicating your concerns. While the harasser is unlikely to reply, you have ensured he is aware of the situation and cannot later claim ignorance. Keep a copy of your letter. For example:

■ Dear Mr Jones,
   On numerous occasions you make personal remarks about my appearance and clothes. You touch me and have made improper suggestions about our work relationship. I find this attention unpleasant and distressing and I am asking you to stop. I would prefer not to take this matter further, but will do so if necessary.

**3.** The harasser may stop if he is aware that other people know about his behaviour. **Ask someone outside work to write a letter**, possibly a relative, doctor or solicitor, outlining your complaint and demanding that the behaviour ceases.

**4.** If your workplace has a **formal complaints (grievance) procedure, use it**. Should your case end up at a tribunal, you will be asked whether or not you informed your employer of the problem (see chapter 7). Your written record will be important here in persuading the personnel or welfare officer to take your case seriously. You will need to overcome initial reactions such as, 'Mr Jones is a family man; he wouldn't do anything like that,' or 'Come on now, a grown woman like you should know how to handle that,' or even 'You can't blame the man for trying.'

**5.** If possible, **ask to discuss the complaint with a woman manager**; while this will not guarantee a sympathetic hearing, women are more likely to know what you are talking about and you may feel more able to speak openly and without embarrassment. In any interview with management, it is a good idea to **take a friend** with you for support; most formal procedures allow you to do this.

**6.** You may eventually be asked to appear at a formal grievance hearing within your workplace, where you should **produce your written evidence** and ask **your witnesses to speak on your behalf**. Members of senior management should hear what you have to say and agree to investigate your complaint.

**7.** You should tell management **what action you want them to take** in dealing with the harasser. You may not only want him to stop harassing you but also to be moved to another job. Alternatively, you may prefer to move. If you offer to do this, make sure your new work situation is **no less favourable** than your previous one.

**8.** Even if there is no formal complaints procedure, you should formally **report your complaint to someone and keep a copy**. If the harasser is your employer, speak to someone else in senior management. If you think they will not understand your complaint, you could take in this book or any other literature to show that other workplaces take the issue seriously.

**9.** Management may well try **to delay investigating your complaint**. They may be unsure about how best to raise it with the harasser; alternatively, from their own observations they may already know your complaint is true but be unwilling to discipline one of their colleagues. To make sure some action is taken, tell management **you will contact them again in a few days** to find out what has happened. Take the same friend with you each time you meet management; this will make it harder for them to go back on any statements they have already made to you.

**10.** Inevitably, your work environment **will be unpleasant while your complaint is investigated**. Management and co-workers may try to persuade you to forget about it; you may also find yourself closely supervised. Wherever possible, talk to your co-workers and friends outside work about what is happening. **Don't give up.** Do not let others convince you the incidents never happened. You know you have been harassed and you have letters and evidence to prove it.

**11.** Hopefully, management will uphold your complaint and take some action against the harasser. **If they do not, you will need to decide what other action**, if any, you want to take. You might try some of the other suggestions outlined in this chapter. If continuing to work with the harasser is making you ill, you may feel the only option is to leave. **Before you make this decision**, read chapter 7 about the law. This explains how you might be able to get compensation for unfair dismissal and sex discrimination for leaving your job due to sexual harassment at work.

## Retaliating

Some women have found the best tactic to stop harassment is to humiliate and embarrass the harasser so that he understands how you feel. However, retaliatory action can make matters worse and should only be tried after careful consideration of all the possible consequences. Retaliation is unwise unless **you have the support and understanding of co-workers**, who will either join in the action or at least accept the reasons for your own behaviour. If you act alone the harasser also may misunderstand your actions for interest in his advances. Should you finally be forced to take your case to the industrial tribunal, your acts of retaliation could be used by your employer to undermine your case.

More generally, retaliation suggests that women complain about harassment only because they are the victims. The long-term answer is not for women to freely harass men. So you should discuss carefully the situations in which retaliation might be appropriate. Some of the ideas which women have tried are:

**1.** When the harasser makes a sexual comment or approach, **speak out loudly so that everyone can hear**, making a remark such as, 'Let's get started then right now,' or 'Fancy you having a hang-up about breasts.' The harasser may be shocked at his behaviour being so publicly acknowledged.

**2.** Talk with co-workers about the harasser's behaviour when he can overhear. Make it obvious you think he is pathetic. **Men hate being laughed at.** When he comes into the work area, get everyone to start laughing and make him feel small.

**3.** **Reverse the harasser's behaviour** so that you behave towards him as he does to you. This could mean putting up pictures of male nudes, making remarks about his appearance, touching his hair or arm, or winking and refusing to treat his remarks about work seriously – by saying, for instance, 'Fancy such a big, husky man like you solving such a difficult problem.'

# Contacting women's groups

Women who are harassed at work experience isolation and a lack of confidence. Even when co-workers are supportive, it may be helpful to make contact with women outside work who are concerned about sexual harassment at work. Over the last few years women's groups and organisations have been set up, some specifically to tackle issues of violence against women, others to offer a general network of discussion and support. All these groups take the view that women need to get together to help themselves overcome the disadvantage and discrimination women experience in society. Joining a group is the best way of developing self-confidence and determination.

**1.** Groups which deal specifically with **violence against women** include Rape Crisis, Women's Aid, and Women Against Violence Against Women (WAVAW). Rape Crisis provides support for women who have been raped or sexually assaulted. Besides legal advice, the group offers counselling on all aspects of sexual abuse. Women are encouraged to talk about their experiences with others and to recognise they are not alone in their feelings of guilt, inadequacy, and anger. Women's Aid provides refuge for women battered by the men they live with and groups exist in most large towns and cities. While not specifically geared to helping women who are sexually harassed at work, they may be able to give you the names of helpful solicitors and local agencies, and put you in contact with other women in your locality. WAVAW is a campaigning group set up to challenge all forms of male violence against women. They run discussion groups, conferences, and put on events around the country to publicise the degree to which women are subjected to violence in their everyday lives. By going along to a meeting, you will be able to find women who support your right to work in a harassment-free workplace.

**2.** Women who work **in particular occupations** have set up women's groups to discuss their experiences of work. While some are very informal, others, such as Women in Libraries, the Radical Midwives and Radical Nurses groups, and Women in Manual Trades have a more formal structure. They meet regularly in some of the major cities, send out newsletters and put on events and conferences. Some, like Women in Manual Trades, are particularly aware of the problem of sexual harassment at work. You might find it helpful to join one of these groups and receive their mailings even if you live some distance from where they meet. You would have someone to contact by phone who shares your work experience and may be able to advise on how best to tackle harassment in your workplace.

3. In most large towns and cities, women have come together to set up their own groups. Some concentrate on **consciousness-raising**, discussing those aspects of society which act to the disadvantage of women and exploring how women themselves unconsciously acquiesce in this process. Others are geared towards **campaigning** on issues important to women such as child-care, abortion, violence, employment, etc. In a few places groups have come together to form a Women's Centre, often running advice and drop-in sessions open to all local women. By contacting a group you may find other women who have experienced harassment and who would welcome an opportunity to talk with you about it.

The addresses of some of the groups mentioned are listed at the end of the book. To find out about groups in your area, contact *Spare Rib*, a monthly women's magazine which lists women's groups in the classified ads section. Or you could phone one of the groups mentioned and ask them to put you in touch with someone. Explain why you want the information. New groups are starting up all the time and there may be one in your area specifically interested in sexual harassment at work.

## Assertiveness and self-defence training

Women are brought up to be nice, passive, and compliant; they are supposed to service other people's needs. At school, for example, girls are not encouraged to be rough and noisy, or to stand up for themselves. When faced with sexual harassment at work, rather than challenge the harasser head-on, women instinctively resort to familiar feminine behaviour by trying to smooth over the issue or ignoring the unpleasantness. A variety of training courses aimed at making women feel strong are now available. While some are offered by private agencies, particularly in the management field, increasing numbers of local authorities are offering courses as part of their adult education programmes. Many are taught by women for women only. These provide opportunities for women to talk about their fears of violence and harassment as well as to practise techniques for dealing with unpleasant or frightening situations. Courses in your area should be advertised in the local paper or adult education brochure; this is usually available from the local library or town hall. For management-based courses, contact the Industrial Society or the National Organisation for Women's Management Education (see Useful Addresses). There are two major types of course:

**1. Self-defence classes** teach a variety of techniques. While some are based on the martial arts like karate and judo, 'women's self-defence' provides basic training for women to cope with a sudden attack. The aim of the course is not to turn women into aggressive street fighters but to build self-confidence through a recognition of a woman's hidden strength. By making women feel positive about themselves and giving them a sense of power, their ability to challenge violence, including harassment at work, is greatly increased.

**2. Assertiveness training** provides an opportunity for women to explore situations in which they feel a lack of confidence. Training programmes are based on a woman's assessment of her own strengths and weakenesses. Practical activities set around both everyday and unusual occurrences at work, such as being confronted by an angry colleague, enable participants to explore different ways of handling tense situations. By developing problem-solving and decision-making skills, women gain confidence in their ability to tackle all types of workplace problems. Having participated in such a course, a women experiencing harassment may find it easier to tackle the harasser and get him to stop.

# 4.

# Organising in the unions

Sexism in trade unions / trade-union policies / workplace procedures / organising for women / helping men / education and training.

Trade unions exist to support their members at work. Over the last century, however, trade-union action has been geared to the needs of male workers, and the demands of their women members have often been ignored, sometimes even suppressed. Women have striven to achieve an equal voice in the labour movement, a struggle which is beginning to show results. Increasing numbers of women are joining trade unions; many unions have national policies to promote equal opportunities and positive action for women members. Issues such as child-care and women's health and safety at work are now on the campaign agenda. The progress achieved by women in securing trade-union recognition of their special needs is highlighted by the relative speed with which sexual harassment at work has been adopted as a legitimate issue for trade-union action. The TUC, together with a number of trade unions, are **formulating policies and procedures** to assist their workplace representatives to deal with members' grievances.

Persuading union activists in the workplace to implement policies beneficial to women members is proving more difficult. Unions fear that tackling issues which expose the sexist attitudes of male workers will create divisions between members, so weakening their ability to challenge the employer. Male workers themselves are afraid of losing their power and status in the workplace if negotiating priorities are redefined in favour of women's demands. As chapter 2 outlines, women's inferior position at work is often the result of sexist practices condoned, and sometimes promoted, by unions. Conflict is bound to arise if men continue to harass women, treating them as playthings and sex-objects rather than as workers. Support for trade-union action from women will be little more than lukewarm unless male trade-union activists acknowledge the different work experiences of women and men. Tackling issues like sexual harassment openly and honestly can only improve the long-term prospects of building trade-union unity between workers.

Even if trade unions prefer to ignore sexual harassment it will not disappear as a workplace problem. Women will expect their union representative to take up specific incidents; unions will have to cope with both harasser and victim as union members; a claim to an industrial tribunal for sex discrimination on the grounds of sexual harassment will require trade-union support. Rather than wait until faced with such a possibility, **unions need to take up the issue now** by developing procedures for dealing with incidents and by combating those practices and attitudes at work which foster harassment. Action at branch and workplace level **must reassure women members** that the union recognises and supports grievances involving sexual harassment. At the same time unions have a responsibility **to help men understand** and overcome their sexist behaviour. Suggestions for trade-union organisation, campaigning and negotiating outlined in the next three chapters indicate ways in which unions might set about this task. This chapter examines:

- **sexism within trade unions;**
- **trade-union policies on sexual harassment;**
- **workplace procedures for tackling sexual harassment;**
- **organising trade unions for women;**
- **helping men understand sexism;**
- **trade-union education on sexism and sexual harassment.**

## Sexism within trade unions

In 1981, 12 million workers were members of a trade union, of whom 30 per cent were women. Women's membership **increased by a million** over the 10 years from 1971, despite the recent high rate of unemployment among women. Male membership over the same period grew more slowly, and has fallen dramatically since 1979 as a consequence of redundancies. Although more women are now members of a trade union, women trade unionists comprise only 41 per cent of the total female workforce; of male workers, 69 per cent are members of a trade union. Within certain unions, however, women make up the majority of members. The narrow range of occupations filled by women results in many of the clerical and service sector unions, such as NUPE and USDAW, being predominantly female unions.

## Table 9: Women in trade unions, 1980 (Coote and Kellner, 1980)

|  | Female membership % | Female executive members % | Female full-time officers % |
|---|---|---|---|
| APEX | 51 | 7 | 4 |
| ASTMS | 17 | 8 | 10.5 |
| BIFU | 49 | 11 | 15 |
| GMWU | 34 | — | 5 |
| NALGO | 50 | 20 | 7 |
| NUPE | 67 | 31 | 5 |
| NUT | 66 | 9 | 15 |
| NUTGW | 92 | 7 | 19 |
| TGWU | 16 | — | 1 |
| USDAW | 63 | 19 | 8 |

High female membership, however, is rarely reflected in the structure of the union. While women may become branch committee members, they seldom fill such posts as branch secretary, chairperson, or regional or divisional delegate. At national level this **under-representation is striking**. As the figures show, few unions have female representation on executive committees equal to their overall membership; in some cases there are no female executive members. A similar situation exists as regards female full-time officers. Under these circumstances, there is inevitably a lack of understanding of women's issues at both policy-making and problem-solving levels in many unions.

This lack of female representation 'where it counts' reflects the problem of developing grass-roots involvement by women in branch and workplace activities. To rise through the structure, women need to gain experience locally. Tackling the low level of membership involvement of both women and men is a priority for all trade unions; increasing women's participation can only be achieved through an understanding of the specific reasons why women find it difficult to become union activists. There is little evidence to suggest that women are less interested than men in trade unions. But to turn that interest into active involvement, **unions need to make themselves more accessible to women**. Jane Stagemen, in a study of women in trade unions, asked women members of five different union branches in the Hull area to outline how women could be encouraged to participate in union activity. Their experiences of trade-union structures and organisation and the sexist attitudes of both husbands and male members kept them from active involvement in union affairs. Of those questioned, 62 per cent said union matters should be easier to understand, 46 per cent asked for opportunities for women to get together and discuss issues of interest to them, and 27 per cent wanted male members to give them a chance to air their views. Other problems limiting their involvement included pressure of domestic responsibilities, lack of confidence, and the time and place of meetings.

Sexism within trade unions takes a number of forms, from the unconscious use of language to overt attempts through collective bargaining to limit women's work opportunities. Trade-union **organisation and procedures developed to suit men**. Communicating involves the 'chairman', 'brothers' and 'yours fraternally'. Speaking at meetings not only demands familiarity with procedures but a willingness to act aggressively in order to be heard. Heckling, shouts of 'point of order' or 'let the motion be put' are enough to deter all but the most hardened activist. Important union business is discussed over a pint after work; branch meetings are held in a pub or trade-union club. Women who want to succeed in the union have to join in, to behave as token men, one of the lads. For many women, their experience of working in the union is of being patronised, called 'dear' or 'luv', rarely being asked for an opinion or having their views taken seriously. Aldred, in *Women at Work*, quotes a woman delegate's report back from a Scottish TUC:

Perhaps most important for me, as a woman trade unionist was the fact that, in a year when the trade-union movement was declaring a positive interest in encouraging increased active participation by female members, it was bemoaning the fact that their 'efforts' in this direction were not showing great results (there were only a handful of women delegates at the conference), it was obvious to me from the outset of the conference that trade unionists must seriously examine the damaging sexist attitudes prevailing at conference. The declaration of women delegates' marital status on the official delegates list; the reference to 'housewives' – not *all* workers – suffering through price rises; and the introduction of the only female platform speaker by referring to her marital and maternal status in the absence of any such references in regard to the male guest speakers, are but a few examples reflecting attitudes all too prevalent in Perth this year.

More obvious forms of sexism also occur. Stageman recalls an USDAW branch meeting where male members left the room as soon as women brought up an issue relevant to them. Marjorie Harrison of ASTMS discovered that some branch secretaries refused to pass on letters from the National Women's Advisory Committee. Others presented one item to a meeting as ' "two women's libbers want to come and talk to you about women's lib", which got the reaction it was geared to receive – rejection'. Knowing that men will not take them seriously, women are reluctant to speak at meetings. Three women trade unionists, talking to Jennie Beale in *Getting it Together*, stated:

> When I'm with men I don't have as much to say as when there is all women, because I don't want to be ridiculed by a man. They tend to make fun of you. I've noticed it. It's wrong, but it's still the attitude. (Angie, TGWU.)
> Your ideas tend to be tolerated but not listened to. Talking in a group the serious remarks tend to be addressed to the men. (Trish, TGWU.)
> My convenor's always going on about equal rights. The other day he said to me, 'What more do you want, you've got equal rights already.' But I've heard him say that he'd have no intention of cooking the dinner. That's his wife's job and the kitchen is no place for him. (Nora, AUEW.)

Sexism within trade unions affects the content of collective agreements. The mechanisms by which women are discriminated against at work, such as job evaluation schemes, sick and seniority pay, terms and conditions for part-time workers, are usually introduced with trade-union involvement. In some cases, trade-union negotiators may be unaware of the indirect disadvantage to women built into such agreements. On other occasions, however, **unions have clearly attempted to restrict women's work opportunities**. During the implementation period for the Equal Pay Act from 1970 to 1975, some unions at local level negotiated bonuses for men or agreed special grades for women in order to help employers circumvent the act.

More recently, women have found their redundancy agreements specify their jobs as first to go. The example of part-time workers at Eley Kynock was quoted in chapter 2; a similar situation occurred in 1982 at Hoovers in Merthyr Tydfil. Since 1970 the semi-skilled grades had been divided into men's and women's jobs, and when management called for 160 redundancies the AUEW asked that the two areas be treated separately. Because of the agreement, women could not transfer to men's jobs. Management decided that 34 per cent of the women and only 8 per cent of the men should go, even though none of the women had worked there for less than eight years, while many of the men had been there only three or four years. The women complained to the Equal Opportunities Commission, asking for their jobs to be integrated and the normal last in, first out principle to apply. The EOC told Hoover its plans were unlawful and Hoover promptly withdrew the redundancies. The company introduced a scheme to integrate men's and women's jobs, in the face of continuing opposition from some union activists.

Trade-union collusion with sexist practices legitimates the attitudes and behaviour of their male members towards women. Many men who harass women are trade-union members. The use of sexual innuendos and comments by male shop stewards when talking to women members is commonplace in many workplaces. Pin-ups and girlie calandars cover the walls of many a convenor's office. At conferences and trade-union residential schools, women activists are subject to sexual abuse and comment. Trade-union journals include sexual remarks about women who may be their own members.

■ **Example:** The February 1983 edition of the TGWU *Record* contained the following items:

Page 5 reported a meeting of the Negotiating Committee of the Scottish and Newcastle bar staff. They were celebrating 10 years of organising what is a notoriously difficult industry to organise. The negotiating committee included a number of women bar staff and women full-time officers.

Page 10 contained a cartoon by the TGWU *Record* 'Underdog' in which the punchline read, 'The closest *he* ever gets to wildlife is the barmaid at the Fox and Hounds.'

Page 11 included a letter from an irate reader complaining about the sexism of a previous 'Underdog' cartoon.

Mostly these incidents go unreported, but one case hit the national headlines. In January 1983 three women members of

SOGAT 82, working for the Mirror Group of newspapers, brought a case under the Sex Discrimination Act on the grounds of victimisation by sexual harassment. The three had been promoted from office cleaning to editorial assistants, jobs traditionally done by men. In their new jobs, they began to receive obscene telephone calls; one woman was assaulted by a drunken colleague; and the men they worked with – all trade-union members – behaved in an abusive and threatening way. Details are sketchy because the case was eventually settled privately just before the tribunal hearing. In the settlement SOGAT 82 and the Daily Mirror both gave undertakings that they would ensure equal opportunities for women and not discriminate against workers on the grounds of sex.

## Trade-union policies

Over the last two years, trade unions have begun developing policies related to sexual harassment. In July 1981, NALGO issued guidelines for members on combating sexual harassment at work, incorporated in a leaflet, 'Sexual harassment is a trade-union issue'. They were immediately inundated with requests for the leaflet from thousands of trade unionists, and distributed over a quarter of a million copies. The 1982 TUC Women's Conference carried a resolution on sexual harassment, proposed by the NUJ and seconded by UCATT:

Conference recognises that sexual harassment is a form of sex discrimination that can damage women trade unionists' morale, job security and prospects at work. It calls on the Women's Advisory Committee to develop guidelines, in consultation with affiliated unions, for reporting and investigating grievances and for dealing with offenders.

Individual unions also debated resolutions at their conferences during 1982. TASS delegates called for a campaign against sexual harassment. The CPSA moved:

Conference is horrified by recent evidence that violence against women is regarded as acceptable and the fault of women themselves, we reject totally the attitude towards women of the judiciary and police, shown in recent rape cases. This Conference believes that in order to combat these attitudes we need to begin in our workplaces with action to counter the problem of sexual harassment at work which is at present often unrecognised or condoned. We call on the NEC to investigate the extent of sexual harassment in our workplaces, and publish a report in *Red Tape* or in an All Member Circular, and include in our union schools discussions on sexual harassment and support any women/men who suffer any sexual harassment at work.

Acting on the conference decision, the TUC Women's Advisory Committee has produced, in consultation with a number of unions, guidelines for dealing with sexual harassment at work. The document, published during August 1983, spells out why sexual harassment is a trade-union issue, what unions should be doing at national, branch and workplace level, and gives advice to individual trade-union members. Unions are urged to produce material about the issue for their members, negotiate procedures with their employer, hold meetings and train representatives to handle individual problems. The guidelines clearly recognise that sexual harassment arises from the inferior position of women at work and that male trade unionists have a responsibility to take the issue seriously. Paragraph 3 states:

> The occurrence of sexual harassment is, in general a product of the position of, and reflects the attitude towards, women in society and in the workplace. Despite the Equal Pay and Sex Discrimination Acts women continue to be confined to the low-paid, semi-skilled, and low-status jobs in service and 'caring' areas, while men predominate in the higher-paid supervisory and skilled jobs. In addition, women's right to play a full role within the workplace is still not rooted firmly in society's attitudes and too often women workers are seen in terms of their family-caring roles or as sexually attractive objects and not as workers attempting to earn their living. The prevalence of this attitude towards women as 'lower status, secondary' workers can foster a situation where a male worker will use his actual or potential power over a female worker to 'keep her in her place'.

Clearly, much work needs to be done to translate all these initiatives into action. With some exceptions, members may not be aware of their union's policy; shop stewards and branch officers will have had little practical experience in tackling the issue. A **local action programme** might well begin as follows:

  1. **Contact your union headquarters** to find out their position

on sexual harassment at work. If they have a policy, **publicise it among your members** prior to organising a meeting. If your union has not yet produced a policy statement, **consider sending a resolution to the next national conference** or through the policy-making structure of your union. You could base a resolution on those illustrated above, calling on the union to draw up practical guidelines to cover the following:

- an investigation into sexual harassment in workplaces associated with the union;
- articles and information in the union newspaper or journal, particularly publicising the TUC guidelines;
- the setting up of an education programme for members and officials;
- a review of grievance and disciplinary procedures to assess their usefulness for dealing with sexual harassment;
- advice to trade-union reps when both harasser and victim are members.

The detailed wording will depend on whether your union negotiates with employers at national or local level. Getting this resolution through the branch **requires careful preparation**. Presented cold, members may well reject it as unnecessary or frivolous. You may prefer, therefore, to **hold a discussion meeting** or publicise some of the factual information in this handbook prior to formally presenting the resolution. Members will need to be convinced that sexual harassment should take precedence over other issues people want debated at a national conference.

   2. **Organise a workplace/branch meeting** to discuss sexual harassment, possibly inviting an outside speaker. Consider the format of the meeting carefully; it is important that members are not embarrassed by the subject matter and feel free to speak. Ideas about meetings will be found later in this chapter and in chapter 5.

   3. Get your branch to pass a resolution **to establish union policy on sexual harassment within your own workplace/area**. This might cover similar items to those applicable at national level, but could also make reference to negotiating policies and procedures with management, examples of which are discussed in chapter 6. The resolution should make it clear that the union locally will support women who are subject to harassment and outline how the union intends to act when the harasser is also a member. In formulating this resolution it is probably a good idea

to include a definition of behaviour that the union considers as sexual harassment. You could adopt either the TUC definition or that proposed by the Working Women's Institute, New York (see pp. 8–9).

**4. Develop an education programme to raise members' awareness** of sexism and sexual harassment. Shop stewards and branch officers should be encouraged to attend training schools in handling cases of sexual harassment. Some ideas for this are included at the end of this chapter. A workplace newsletter or leaflet could be used as the basis of section meetings and discussions, as well as giving advice on what action to take if a member experiences harassment.

Once the action programme is underway, branches and workplace committees would be able to consider some of the campaigning ideas discussed in chapter 5.

## Workplace procedures

Trade-union members and representatives need guidance on handling cases of sexual harassment at work. Ideally, complaints of harassment by a co-worker or superior should be treated in the same way as any other workplace problem. However, given the sensitivity of the subject, **unions should discuss how they want to handle harassment cases**. Unless the membership is informed that sexual harassment is a trade-union issue, few women will approach the union with a complaint but instead try to cope with it by themselves. Men in the workplace must be made aware of trade-union policy and be given guidance on the behaviour and remarks which could cause offence. Shop stewards and safety representatives need training in the range of trade-union issues associated with cases of sexual harassment so they can investigate complaints both sympathetically and thoroughly. Unions should make it clear to managements that they intend to deal with cases through workplace procedures; it may also be useful to negotiate a management policy and training programme on the issue (see chapter 6). Sorting out procedures **in advance of a case is essential** if unions are to avoid making hasty judgements. Trade unions have particular problems where both victim and harasser are members of the same union. Two examples illustrate some of these difficulties.

■ **Example:** Three women NALGO members working for Bren Council complained to the assistant branch secretary about persistent sexual harassment by a senior officer of the council. The union representative reported the complaint to management, who required further evidence, which the representative started to collect. The senior officer, also a NALGO member, heard about the complaint and, supported by the branch secretary, approached NALGO for legal backing. Libel writs were issued by NALGO head office against the union representatives dealing with the women's case. The local NALGO branch voted overwhelmingly to support the women.

Prior to holding an enquiry, management suspended everyone involved, including the union representatives. The enquiry decided the allegations were unfounded and the women were asked to retract their complaints and apologise. They refused. While not taking formal disciplinary action, the women were moved to lower-status jobs. (*Spare Rib*, September 1979.)

[The outcry throughout the country about the way NALGO handled the case prompted the union to examine the general problem of sexual harassment and to issue their leaflet.]

◀ **Example:** In 1981 two women members of the TGWU working in the canteen of an engineering company complained about the behaviour of the head chef, also a TGWU member. He was dismissed by the company for sexual harassment. The man approached the union for help, and the district officer agreed to attend the appeal hearing to check that the disciplinary procedure was properly applied.

The sacking was upheld and the man asked the union to support a claim of unfair dismissal. The union advised him of his rights and how to make the tribunal application. The TGWU was not, however, prepared to fight the case because the evidence of sexual harassment was overwhelming and their women members in the canteen had wanted action taken against the harasser. (Sedley and Benn, p. 27.)

While such situations can present conflicts of interest for a union, there are many occasions when problems between members have to be dealt with. Fighting, verbal abuse and personality clashes between members, and bad work affecting other members' bonus payments, are all examples of issues which shop stewards regularly take up. In some instances, the problems are resolved **by discussion between members and the union**; in others, management may become involved. Depending on the circumstances, the union may support both members, where, for example, management are over-reacting to a personal disagreement. Where the membership is firmly of the opinion that one side deserves support, the other member(s) should simply be given information about their rights and a check made to ensure proper procedures are used. With experience, most stewards know when a member has exhausted union support.

Arrangements for dealing with cases of sexual harassment between members need to be clearly understood. Providing the union has made its policy available to all members, and discussed with them its implications, then any member who persists in harassing others is likely to lose union support. Some unions are prepared to implement their policy of withdrawing union membership from anyone whose conduct is against the interests of the union. Such drastic steps should obviously only be considered in extreme circumstances. To prevent reaching this situation, unions need to discuss how male members can be helped to understand that their behaviour and attitudes cause offence. Some ideas on this will be found later in the chapter.

Following discussion, unions need to issue advice to their representatives and members on how to take up sexual harassment cases. You can use the guidelines below as the basis of a trade-union procedure for your workplace, which should be circulated to all members.

## Advice to shop stewards/safety representatives

**1. Inform yourself** of the trade-union issues associated with sexual harassment at work. A member may come to you about something else when her real problem is connected with harassment. Stress, poor work performance, refusal to undertake certain tasks, disciplinary problems, could all be related to sexual harassment. You will need to approach these issues sensitively, since your member has not mentioned them.

**2.** When a member comes to you with a complaint of sexual harassment, **listen sympathetically**. Remember, it is very difficult for a victim to report the incident. She does not know how you will react so be straightforward and show you are not embarrassed or annoyed by her complaint. Be aware that your first reaction could be to prejudge the victim and blame her for the incident or for being unable to cope.

**3. Reassure the woman** that her problem will be taken seri-

ously. **Find out what she wants done.** Is she looking for the union
to discuss the matter directly with the harasser if he is a co-
worker? If management is involved, does she want to lodge a
formal complaint? Explain to her that the union wants to help
solve these kinds of problems.

4. **Start to build a case.** You should ask the victim to keep a
record, including time, place and details of each incident. Try to
find witnesses. This may be difficult because so much harassment
occurs in private. If other members are reluctant to speak, reassure them that the union will protect them from victimisation.
If you can, find out if other women have also experienced harassment from this particular man. (You may like to include details
about keeping a diary in your procedure – see chapter 3.)

5. **Keep the information confidential** until you are ready to
prove the case. The woman may feel guilty or worried about how
others will react once her complaint is known. Do not alert the
harasser until you are ready to take up the issue formally, or he
may lodge a counter-complaint.

6. Once you have sufficient information, **sort out what action
to take**. You will need to discuss this with the victim, and maybe
with other shop stewards. If the harasser is a union member,
decide whether you should deal with the complaint informally
first.

7. If you decide to take the case through **formal grievance
procedure**, make sure the branch/shop stewards committee
agrees. If necessary, inform your full-time official.

## Advice to members

1. **The union is concerned to support members** who experience
sexual harassment from a co-worker or superior. Sexual harassment does not go away if it is ignored. If you do nothing, the
harasser may think you do not mind his behaviour. But in the
long run you may find harassment affects your work. **So seek help
and speak to your union representative.**

2. **Sexual harassment is not your fault**; it is the harasser who is
in the wrong. In order to justify his behaviour, the harasser may
accuse you of 'asking for it'. But **you should not feel guilty** about
your dress or personal appearance.

3. Your steward can help you sort out the problem, either by
approaching the harasser or by taking up a formal complaint. But
even if you do not want anything done about it, **report it to the**

**union.** You may find they already have other complaints or can find ways of dealing with the problem which keeps it confidential.

**4.** Your steward will ask you to **keep a record of each incident** – time, date and what happened. Check if there were any witnesses. This may be useful later.

**5.** With the help of the union, make a **record of your work**, particularly if you have been complimented for good work. Check your absentee and sickness record. This will ensure management cannot use poor work performance as an excuse to get rid of you. The union will protect you from victimisation.

**6.** Find out if any other women are harassed by this man. Mention the problem to other people you work with. Many women do not complain because they are afraid of victimisation or of being blamed. Let them know that **by sticking together and with union support, the problem can be resolved**.

In drawing up a workplace procedure, unions should consider who is best able to handle cases. Unions may prefer the section or group steward to take up the case in the normal way. However, it is advisable for unions to **designate one or two representatives**, preferably women, to deal with all sexual harassment cases, at least in the first instance. Not all male shop stewards or safety reps will feel comfortable discussing the issue with women members; women may themselves be reluctant to speak to a man. Another woman is more able to understand the feelings of the victim and provide helpful support. Recognising this, some unions have agreed that complaints are referred to the branch or workplace **equal opportunities committee**, which would look into the case. At any formal hearing with management, the victim would be supported by both her shop steward and a member of the committee.

## Organising for women

Workplace procedures are only effective for taking up specific incidents of harassment. To tackle the broader aspects of sexism within the workplace and union structure, **trade-union organisation must be changed**. The TUC *Charter on Equality for Women within Trade Unions* goes some way towards making unions more accessible to women. A number of its proposals aim to increase the participation of women at policy-making levels including the setting up of special advisory committees and reserved seats for women. At branch and workplace level, unions

re asked to examine the time of meetings, the availability of
hild-care so that women can attend meetings, and special train-
ng courses for women members. Point 10 of the charter asks
nions to check the language of union publications to ensure it
either excludes women nor refers to them in sexist terms.

## UC Charter on Equality for Women within Trade Unions

1. The National Executive Committee of the union should publicly declare to all its members the commitment of the union to involving women members in the activities of the union at all levels.

2. The structure of the union should be examined to see whether it prevents women from reaching the decision-making bodies.

3. Where there are large women's memberships but no women on the decision-making bodies special provision should be made to ensure that women's views are represented, either through the creation of additional seats or by co-option.

4. The National Executive Committee of each union should consider the desirability of setting up advisory committees within its constitutional machinery to ensure that the special interests of its women members are protected.

5. Similar committees at regional, divisional, and district level could also assist by encouraging the active involvement of women in the general activities of the union.

6. Efforts should be made to include in collective agreements provision for time off without loss of pay to attend branch meetings during working hours where that is practicable.

7. Where it is not practicable to hold meetings during working hours every effort should be made to provide child-care facilities for use by either parent.

8. Child-care facilities, for use by either parent, should be provided at all district, divisional and regional meetings and particularly at the union's annual conference, and for training courses organised by the union.

9. Although it may be open to any members of either sex to go to union training courses, special encouragement should be given to women to attend.

10. The content of journals and other union publications should be presented in non-sexist terms.

While the charter represents an advance for women, not a
unions are vigorously implementing its proposals. At the sam
time it omits the single organisational change most likely to brin
women into active membership – **the setting-up of women-onl
union meetings**.

Women-only meetings are already established practice i
some unions. For the last two years, the TUC education servic
has been running women-only courses, with women tutors. Fo
lowing a motion on sexual harassment at their 1982 conference
the SCPS organised women-only seminars around the country i
order to initiate discussion on the issue. Yet some unions ar
either sceptical or positively opposed to such a development, fc
fear of dividing their membership and alienating men within th
union. In supporting this view, unions fail to take account of th
high level of dissatisfaction with union organisation which is fe
by many of their women members. In the Hull survey describe
earlier, 46 per cent of women said they would welcome th
opportunity of meeting without men. Where women are able t
get together, all the evidence points to their increased intere
and involvement in union affairs. In *Hear this, Brother*, Ann
Coote reported on her visit to a NUPE weekend school fc
women members:

> I recently visited a NUPE weekend school, arriving on Sunda
> afternoon after 25 women – nurses, caterers, cleaners, a roa
> sweeper, a gardener and others – had been together for 3
> hours . . . It wasn't just that they'd had a good time, althoug
> that was important enough; they'd spent the daytime learnin
> how to negotiate and discussing their common and separat
> experiences. They had evidently found it invaluable. No
> they said they wanted more courses like this one; they wante
> to learn more and they wanted to see each other again. 'W
> couldn't have spoken freely if men had been here.' 'We need
> few more of these, and then we could go on a mixed course.'

But occasional training courses are not enough. Few women ca
afford the time away from home; meetings need to be hel
regularly if self-confidence and enthusiasm are to be maintainec
Women within a particular branch or workplace should have th
opportunity to get together to discuss common problems, nc
only on issues specific to women but also to examine how genera
policies affect women members. **Women-only meetings ar
essential** if women are to discuss their experiences of sexua

harassment and sexism at work. Fear of being laughed at in a mixed meeting, of being aggressively challenged by men to prove it, even the possibility that the harasser could be present, would turn the meeting into a nightmare for any woman wanting to discuss her problem. As a result, she would remain silent, and the problem remain hidden.

Women-only meetings can offer a friendly, supportive environment where ideas and feelings may be explored before being taken up in a more formal setting. Without this opportunity, there is little chance of women talking openly about their experiences of sexism; without this input, trade-union policies and procedures could remain empty gestures.

## Helping men understand sexism

To support women, trade unions face the major task of challenging sexism in the workplace. Unions are not in the business of getting men disciplined for behaviour and attitudes which are part of everyday life. At the same time, men must be aware that sexist practices, including sexual harassment, humiliate women, undermine their self-confidence and place their sex above their competence as a worker. As illustrated in the next chapter, one way of raising awareness is to campaign around specific issues by a workplace questionnaire or pin-up campaign. Unions could, however, also consider ways in which men may help each other sort out their attitudes and behaviour towards women. Little practical experience of doing this is as yet available within the trade-union movement; nevertheless, a number of options could be pursued.

1. **Providing a counselling service** for members who practise sexual harassment. Some unions in the USA and Australia have developed formal counselling procedures to be used prior to any disciplinary action being taken. Where there is evidence of sexual harassment against a member, he is advised to attend a series of discussion sessions with one or two designated trade-union representatives to talk through his behaviour. This may continue regularly until the union is satisfied that he both understands the issues and is prepared to stop the harassment. In some cases, members must attend if they want to avoid a formal complaint being lodged against them. To offer such a service, unions need to train representatives in the broad range of issues related to sexual harassment. Reps must be sensitive to the difficulties faced by their member while remaining firmly committed to

challenging sexist practices. Unions need to decide whethe counsellors should include women as well as men. Men may find it easier to talk with other men; perhaps it's important for the harasser to understand how women feel about his behaviour?

**2.** Asking male members to **actively combat sexism** within their workplace. While not all men at work harass women o treat them as sex-objects, few men actually challenge the lan guage and behaviour of those that do. Rather than colluding with harassment, by feeling that 'men should stick together', male workers must be encouraged to identify sexist practices and support women who complain of harassment. They should tackle co-workers who talk about women in an offensive way or bring pornographic magazines to work. By taking up these issues, men will begin to show those they work with that not all men agree with traditional patterns of male behaviour. Workplace discus sions or branch training sessions will help men develop the confidence to take up this challenge.

**3.** Creating opportunities for **men to explore their own feel ings and their attitudes towards women**. In the long run, change in the way men treat women may only come when men recognis that traditional masculine behaviour can be positively harmfu not only to women but to themselves. Jon Cook, in a *New Statesman* article about 'Sex and Socialism', argued:

> Change here means learning; and it is men who have the mos to learn. We could begin by recognising that the spectre c male sexuality doesn't only menace women, but messes us u too. The sexual code promoted by the fantasy images c *Playboy*, or page three of the *Sun*, cultivates a notion tha men's sexual relations with women are to be defined in term of success or failure. Success means mastery.
>
> But talking about change in this area is easier than actuall changing. In the case of men we shall have to dredge up thos parts of our past which the very obsession with sexual succes and failure have suppressed. This will mean, among othe things, unlearning men's reticence about personal feeling which our own culture defines as a sign of masculine authorit The conditions for such a process of change cannot be found i parliamentary debates or mass meetings but in some therapeut practice which will be conscious of its wider political obligation

At present, there are almost no opportunities within the stru ture of trade unions for men to talk about their feelings toward women or to explore, for example, the conflict between being trade-union activists and wanting to be involved in their children's upbringing. Union training schools and education courses do, however, provide one possible forum for discussing the nature of masculinity. Doug Miller, writing in *Trade Union Studies Journal* (Winter 1982), outlines his own experiences as a tutor of raising the issue on shop stewards' training courses. He argues that a group of men meeting regularly together may eventually feel the degree of safety necessary to explore how it feels to be a man. He concludes that while not offering 'a direct blow against sexism, the prospect of men becoming . . . more open . . . through their experience-sharing would make a decisive start in contradicting many of the behaviour patterns which are commonplace inside and outside trade unions today.'

Many women as well as men remain sceptical as to how far such discussions can begin to change men's sexist attitudes and behaviour. In addition, union activists may not view with favour the idea of men sitting down together to discuss personal experiences; with so many pressing issues to tackle, finding the time for self-examination can seem an unnecessary luxury. On the other hand, sexist practices present a major limitation to involving more women in trade-union activity. Changing the personal relationships between women and men at work is an integral part of building a united labour movement. Unions need to find ways of ensuring men take responsibility for their own behaviour by raising the issue within their education programmes at branch, district and national levels.

## Education and training

Effective action aimed at tackling sexual harassment at work depends on trade-union activists and members being aware of the issues. While producing a leaflet or holding a meeting are important first steps, these initiatives should be taken **in conjunction with an education programme**. In particular, trade-union reps need to feel confident about dealing with members' complaints and explaining why harassment is a trade-union issue. Already, a number of unions run training schools for women members as well as including women's issues as part of their education programme for both lay and full-time officers. Courses offered by the TUC Education Service through local colleges and the Workers' Educational Association also provide an opportunity to discuss issues relating to sexism and sexual harassment.

One union, the SCPS, has run a series of two-day seminars fo women representatives in different parts of the country so tha they in turn can organise women-only branch meetings on sexua harassment. A special pack of training materials has been pro duced to support the activity.

Schools, courses and discussion meetings are vital if trade union reps and members are to understand not only how to dea with harassment when it occurs but also to identify and comba sexist attitudes and practices which support harassment. Union need to look for opportunities to raise the issue within thei training programmes for lay and full-time officers. Such trainin needs to cover a number of topics:

- what is sexual harassment;
- trade-union approach to sexual harassment;
- handling members' complaints;
- counselling the harasser;
- workplace campaigning against sexism and sexual harass ment.

To help generate ideas for such a programme, a number c discussion activities are included at the end of this chapter. Thei purpose is to promote an exchange of ideas between trade unior ists on a broad range of issues related to sexism and sexua harassment. The activities explore attitudes and workplac practices as well as including problem-solving case studies. The can be adapted or extended to suit the needs of a particular unio or workplace, and may be used at a union weekend school c over a series of branch/workplace meetings.

The format of the discussion needs careful planning. Eac activity is designed for a small group of three or four trade-unio members/reps, followed by a report-back to the larger grour For some activities it may be more appropriate to divide grour according to sex, and then compare the responses of women an men. For others, mixed groups may be more useful. Grour might also be arranged according to the type or size of work place. The report-back session can be informal or taken as part c a union meeting; case studies can be adapted as an interviewin exercise or negotiating role-play. The questionnaire in chapte 5 is also a useful way of getting members to think about sexua harassment, either by filling it in themselves, or using it to dra up a questionnaire for use in their own workplace.

Whether or not the material in this handbook is used, th

content of an education programme about sexism and sexual harassment needs to include activities which explore members' own attitudes as well as those involving case studies and workplace problems. Without such a discussion, union reps can end up dealing with other people's problems without understanding their own sexist attitudes and behaviour. It is only by reps 'practising what they preach' that members who experience sexual harassment will trust the union's ability to take up their complaint successfully.

## Hints on using the activities

*Activity 1: Workplace survey*   The purpose of this survey is to help reps/members to identify sexist practices within their workplace. Alternatively, some of the questions could be adapted for a survey of the union branch.

**1.** Ask reps/members to complete the survey before attending the discussion session.

**2.** Within small groups, compare different workplaces, or ask reps from the same workplace to prepare a report using the survey information.

**3.** Identify problem-areas and discuss their possible causes.

**4.** Ask reps/members to draw up an action programme to tackle the problems.

*Activity 2: Views about women and men*   This activity explores how union reps/members see women and men. It offers an opportunity to discuss:

- how far women and men are seen as different;
- how each sex is brought up to be women and men;
- which personality characteristics are usually considered 'good' and 'bad';
- how far traditional sex-stereotyped views of men and women reflect reality.

**1.** Divide the larger group either into single-sex groups or mixed groups depending on how you want to structure the later discussion.

**2.** *Either:* ask each person to fill in the checklist as they think, and then go through it with their group to identify a group view; *or* ask the small group to discuss each characteristic before coming to a group view. Ask the group to jot down any examples or comments to back up their views, preferably taken from their experiences at work.

**3.** Take a report-back from each group and examine the similarities/differences between groups. Link this to the inferior status of women at work.

*Activity 3: Trade-union approaches to sexism*   This activity explores reps'/members' attitudes to sexist practices in the workplace. It should encourage an exchange of views about workplace relationships between women and men, and the role of the trade union in combating sexism.

**1.** Ask the small groups to discuss each statement and jot down their comments, before coming to a view.

**2.** Take report-back from groups, identifying similarities/differences, ideas for action, and possible problem-areas for further discussion.

**3.** Go on to examine any ideas for action and ask participants to draw up more detailed proposals about combating sexist attitudes in their workplace.

*Activity 4: Handling problems*   This activity includes a number of workplace problems associated with sexism and sexual harassment. In talking through the issues, reps/members will need to sort out:

- their attitudes to the problem;
- the role of the trade union in taking up the issue;
- possible plan of action.

**1.** Ask each small group to prepare a report for a union branch/workplace meeting examining the issues and if appropriate, proposing a plan of action.

**2.** Hold a union branch/workplace committee meeting to discuss the reports and decide on trade-union action.

*Activity 5: Dealing with sexual harassment*   These four case studies raise a range of issues related to individual complaints about sexual harassment. They can be used for:

- an interviewing exercise between member and union rep;
- a report to a workplace committee on possible trade-union action;
- background to drawing up workplace procedures and policy for dealing with sexual harassment;
- a negotiating role-play following a formal complaint to management;
- sorting out how to deal with a complaint when the harasser is a trade-union member.

## Activity 1: Workplace survey

Complete the following information about your workplace and use the results to discuss issues of women, sexism and trade unions:

1. Number employed:  Men .............. Women ..........
   Number in a trade union:  Men .............. Women ..........
   Number of trade-union reps:  Men .............. Women ..........

2. List the sections/occupations within your workplace where women outnumber men. What proportion of trade-union reps in these sections are women?

3. List the sections/occupations within your workplace where men outnumber women. What proportion of trade-union reps in these sections are women?

4. Examine the occupational/grading structure of your workplace. What proportion of women are in each grade? Where in the structure do you find most women?

5. Walk around your workplace/section and note down the location of any pin-ups, girlie calendars, etc.

6. Are any of the following terms used by men to address women in your workplace? Luv, gorgeous, dear, sexy.

7. Do men ever whistle or catcall at women in your workplace?

8. Has your union negotiated an equal opportunities policy with your employer? If no, why not? If yes, what discussions have taken place to ensure the practical implementation of the policy?

9. When, if ever, has your union workplace committee discussed any of the following issues which particularly affect women at work:
   - child-care provision;
   - women's health at work;
   - sex bias in job evaluation/grading schemes;
   - recruitment policies;
   - positive action programme;
   - sexual harassment;
   - union organisation and facilities for women members.

10. Are there any opportunities in your workplace/union branch for women to meet together to discuss workplace issues?

## Activity 2: Views about women and men

In a small group, discuss the personality characteristics listed below. Indicate which characteristics the group consider are more typical of each sex.

|  | Mainly men | Mainly women | Found equally in both |
|---|---|---|---|
| Not very aggressive | | | |
| Independent-minded | | | |
| Rather emotional | | | |
| Not easily influenced by others | | | |
| Excitable in a minor crisis | | | |
| Not very competitive | | | |
| Cannot make decisions easily | | | |
| Personally ambitious | | | |
| Interested in own appearance | | | |
| Express tender feelings easily | | | |
| Insensitive to others | | | |
| Lacks self-confidence | | | |
| Likes to dominate a situation | | | |
| Enjoys solving problems | | | |
| Interested mainly in home and family | | | |

## Activity 3: Trade-union approaches to sexism

In small groups, discuss the following statements. Indicate how far you agree or disagree with them, noting down your comments.

1. Unions have no right to tell members to remove pin-ups from the workplace.

2. Discussing sexual harassment with members will open up divisions between men and women in the union.

3. Calling a woman co-worker 'gorgeous' or 'sexy' is just being friendly.

4. Women are their own worst enemies because they are not interested in taking on more responsible/skilled jobs.

5. Men are unwilling/unhappy to be supervised by a woman.

6. Positive action programmes discriminate against men.

## Activity 4: Handling problems

The following problems have been reported to your union workplace committee. How would you want to deal with them?

1. You have heard that the works social club intends putting on a strip show at the request of a number of workers, who are union members.

2. A woman member comes to you complaining about the nude pin-ups in the foreman/supervisor's office.

3. A number of women members have refused to walk through the ware-house because of the whistling and catcalls they receive.

4. A woman member reports she is being pestered by a co-worker on the way home.

5. Your workplace committee agreed that women members should hold their own meeting to discuss the issue of sexual harassment. A group of male members have now complained that they should be allowed to go as well.

## Activity 5: Dealing with sexual harassment

### Case study 1

You are a shop steward in a small factory making electronic components. One of your members, Mary Jones, has told you she is thinking of lodging a formal complaint because she is fed up with the attentions of one of the male technicians. On several occasions he has followed her towards the toilets, asked her personal questions about her private life and frequently stared at her. Last week when he spoke to her he momentarily touched her breast. She says his attentions are affecting her work. Both are members of your union. What actions would you take to deal with this problem?

### Case study 2

You are shop steward in the leisure services department of a local authority. Marion Reed, a senior clerical worker in the section, has asked to see you as she is interested in being promoted to an administrative post. She tells you that on several occasions when she has to work in the office of one of the department officers, he has delayed her in conversation, remarked about her clothes and appearance, and has twice put his arm round her. Most recently he has suggested she would do well in an administrative post and mentioned that a vacancy was likely in the near future. He suggested they talk about it further and have lunch together. Marion wants to apply for the job but is concerned that the department officer would be involved in the interview. She wants your advice. The officer is a member of another union.

### Case study 3

You are a shop steward in a large department stores. Audrey Wright, one of the assistants working in the kitchenware section in the basement, has come to you because she is about to be given a verbal warning for bad timekeeping, faults in her work, and a poor sickness record. She seems a nervous person, constantly on the brink of tears, and considering leaving her job. She had no problems until six months ago when she was transferred to the basement.

The basement houses a number of departments where the assistants and floor managers are mostly men. On talking to Audrey you discover that she finds her working environment unpleasant, with lots of innuendos and lewd jokes, and that several of the men have brought in pornographic magazines and discussed them in her hearing. She is embarrassed and feels on her own because the rest of the women staff, who are younger than her, find it a joke and consider her a bit of a prude. Several months ago at a staff party one of the floor managers grabbed her in a corridor and tried to kiss her. She struggled to get away and told him how she felt. Since then he has made her the focus of jokes and loudly discussed the incident with others.

Audrey is worried about the disciplinary hearing and is unsure about bringing up these issues. She thinks it may be easier to leave. The floor manager is strongly anti-union.

## Activity 5: Dealing with sexual harassment *(continued)*

**Case study 4**

With a number of other stewards from your workplace, you are attending a residential training school organised by your union. Of the 50 stewards present, only seven are women.

On the third morning of the course, Jean Smith, who is one of the stewards from your workplace, comes to see you before breakfast. She is very upset. She says that the previous night one of the men attending the course had had too much to drink and started to pester her. She decided to leave and go to bed, but as she went out of the room, the man followed her, making suggestions about their sleeping together which were loud enough for everyone to hear. She hurried to her room, locked herself in, and tried to sleep.

She tells you she cannot face the embarrassment of going to breakfast and that the course has been spoiled for her. As the man involved is in her discussion group, she thinks it would be better if she went home. She wants you to apologise to the course organisers on her behalf.

# 5.

# Workplace campaigns

Campaigning against pin-ups / workplace questionnaire / meetings / publicity.

Sexual harassment will remain a workplace problem until traditional male attitudes and behaviour towards women undergo
fundamental change. Achieving such changes requires **a long and
persistent campaign** among people at work to both identify and
challenge sexist practices. While unions are developing policies
dealing with sexual harassment, little discussion is as yet taking
place about ways of implementing policy at branch and workplace level. This inaction arises not only from a lack of information and understanding about the issues, but also from an uncer-
tainty within unions as to the most appropriate ways of raising
questions about people's behaviour which have always been
regarded as a personal and private matter.

Yet campaigning around sexism and sexual harassment is no
different from many other union activities. Trade unions have
considerable experience in raising membership awareness of
issues which members do not automatically associate with the
union. Campaigns about cuts in public expenditure, social security benefits, racism and government economic policy inevitably
highlight members' attitudes towards claimants, public sector
workers and black people. Few activists doubt the long-term
importance to the trade-union movement of vigorously pursuing
these issues even though such campaigns have not yet succeeded
in winning the support of the entire trade-union membership. No
campaign will get off the ground if unions wait until all members
are sympathetic or the perfect strategy has been agreed. Much of
the success in changing attitudes has come from developing these
campaigns in ways that reflect the interest and experiences of the
members involved.

This chapter looks at the experiences of two types of union

campaign – **action to remove pin-ups** and **a workplace questionnaire on sexual harassment**. Neither example is a blueprint for other unions; however, the success of these actions may give ideas and encouragement to those interested in taking up sexism and sexual harassment within their branch or workplace. The form and content of any campaign must depend on the membership – a workplace comprising mainly men will need to develop a different approach to one where women are in a majority. A small workplace can rely on informal contacts and discussion; a larger workplace requires printed publicity and special meetings. Some hints on both **meetings** and **publicity** can be found at the end of the chapter. Any union committee starting a campaign will need to consider the following.

### Aims of the campaign

Do not be over-ambitious in the first instance. You will not succeed in removing every pin-up or sexist remark overnight. Informing the membership about sexual harassment or finding out if harassment is a problem in your workplace may be an essential first step. The aim may change as the campaign develops; both examples given here illustrate how new ideas and issues arose from the initial activity.

### Using the trade-union structure

Members and management will almost certainly take more notice of the campaign if it is backed by the formal union structures at the workplace. In the two examples discussed in this chapter, the initiative for the pin-up campaign came from the senior stewards committee, and for the questionnaire, the equal opportunities committee of the branch obtained branch approval for their campaign. Convincing the shop stewards committee or a branch meeting can therefore be the most important single action of the campaign; so marshal your arguments carefully and do not give up at the first rebuff.

### Collecting relevant information

Convincing your members that sexism and sexual harassment are trade-union issues will be an essential part of any campaign. Sort out the information you need:

- union policies on equal opportunities, positive action, sexual harassment;
- examples of sexual harassment which are relevant to your workplace;

- facts and figures about the incidence of harassment and its consequences for women workers;
- the main arguments you want to use with your members;
- possible counter-arguments from your members and how you want to deal with them.

## Building membership support

The main thrust of the campaign is likely to be aimed at changing the attitudes and behaviour of male members and to give women members confidence that the union takes their needs seriously. Whatever the specific aims of the campaign, you will probably need to:

- find as many opportunities as possible for informal discussion with members, where they can talk through the issues and sort out their own ideas;
- hold workplace/section meetings to discuss aspects of the campaign and report on progress;
- produce some publicity about the campaign, such as leaflets, a newsletter, minutes of meetings, posters;
- examine ways of involving all members in some activity within the workplace, like a questionnaire, or talk with section steward.

## Involving management

Not all campaigns will require the union to approach management since the main aim may be to build awareness of sexism among the members. You will need to decide whether or not it is necessary, and if so, at what stage. Bear in mind:

- any workplace campaign may lead management to query the way the union is using its time-off agreement. You need to argue that the campaign is relevant to industrial relations in the workplace;
- campaigns about sensitive issues may cause some raised eyebrows, both inside and outside the workplace. Management may need to be forewarned of this possibility. In the examples in this chapter, local newspapers latched onto and sensationalised the campaigns;
- a successful campaign may encourage women to make complaints of harassment which need to be taken up through the grievance procedures; it could be useful to discuss this possibility with management before it happens;

- as the campaign develops, you may want to approach management to negotiate a workplace policy on equal opportunities and sexual harassment.

*Taking action*

Not all campaigns involve industrial action by unions to support policy. However, if specific issues are formally taken to management through normal negotiating channels, unions need to consider appropriate forms of action to back up their demands. Since sexism and sexual harassment are new issues for members, careful discussion is needed about when and how to exert pressure if management are proving unco-operative.

# Campaigning against pin-ups

Around 1,700 workers are employed in the direct labour organisation (DLO) of Sandwell district council, in the West Midlands. With the exception of a handful of cleaners, all the workers are men – carpenters, bricklayers, plumbers, electricians, painters and decorators, working from a series of depots and sites in the area. All are members of a union, of which there are six – TGWU, EEPTU, GMBATU, FTAT, UCATT, and NUPE. The joint stewards committee, responsible for negotiating with management, comprises the senior stewards of each union; senior stewards report back to single-union stewards committees, who have stewards on each site. The DLO has a history of involvement in broad campaigns – in the local anti-racist group, by affiliating to CND, and through joint action with council tenants. In 1980, the senior stewards committee launched a campaign against pin-ups in the site and depot offices.

## Getting started

The campaign was prompted by a combination of factors.

1. Senior stewards visiting sites and depots to talk to members noticed increasing numbers of pin-ups, hard and soft porn photos, and obscene graffiti depicting women's bodies on the office walls.

2. Women cleaners began to grumble informally about the pictures and graffiti in areas where they cleaned; one woman steward in particular began questioning why women had to work in such an environment.

3. Senior stewards attending meetings with management at

the central depot noticed pin-ups in management offices; in many cases these had been defaced with added drawings and comments. In one office where half the workers were women, one wall was completely covered with such pictures.

**4.** While waiting to see management, stewards would chat to women in the various offices. They found some of the women felt humiliated by being compared to the pictures; in addition, the younger women in one office were frequently harassed by two managers but were too terrified to complain. Union organisation in the offices was weak.

**5.** In October of each year, the DLO was deluged with calendars from suppliers interested in winning orders from the council. Senior stewards were aware that managers put in requests for specific calendars, the most senior managers having first pick of the pin-ups.

### Convincing the membership

**1.** The issue was first raised at a senior stewards meeting. Initially only three stewards accepted that pin-ups were a trade-union issue. As with other workplace campaigns, the senior stewards committee held **many meetings debating the proposed action**. Eventually they agreed to seek support for a campaign; similar discussions then took place within each union committee. Informal discussions were started with the members. Finally, all the unions agreed to campaign for the removal of pin-ups and other pictures from all the working areas used by members of the manual unions.

**2.** Taking the issue to the members involved weeks of informal and formal site meetings, at which stewards pressed for the removal of all pin-ups. Given the few women working in these areas, most of the arguments were between male stewards and members. In convincing the membership to support the policy, the unions pointed out:

- the pictures/drawings were upsetting the women cleaners who had to work there; the union must support members who complained about unpleasant working conditions;
- the pictures/drawings undermined the ability of women to do their job properly because of unsatisfactory working conditions; men rightly complained if fellow workers or a foreman 'put them down' so they should support similar action on behalf of women;

- the union should put its equal opportunities policy into practice by treating women with respect and ensuring equality at work;
- the men would not like their wives or daughters to work in such an environment or be compared with the pictures so why should other women have to put up with it;
- the pictures/drawings constituted sexual harassment because they degraded women by taunting them with unpleasant images;
- the stewards' objections to the pictures were not on the grounds of prudery; it was not a question of the exact pose or lack of clothing but the display of the female body which degraded and humiliated women.

**3.** Not surprisingly, members took time to be convinced. In the early stages of the campaign, **a minority of members actively opposed** the stewards' action. Their arguments and actions included:

- attempting to undermine membership respect for the stewards by questioning their masculinity, calling them soft, gay, weird, screwed up;
- presenting the issue as about the freedom of the individual to do as he liked and not a suitable issue for trade-union policy;
- complaining to the union district office about one steward for wasting union time on a trivial matter;
- refusing outright to take down the pictures, coupled with threats of physical violence if they were touched;
- attempting to goad the stewards by deliberately putting up pictures when they were due to visit a site; also trying to cause trouble between a steward and some of the younger women at the depot offices by engineering awkward situations.

Despite these difficulties, this first stage of the campaign was successful. The pictures were removed, and the defaced walls were whitewashed. By refusing to rise to the bait or to neglect other workplace issues, none of the stewards lost the support of their members. **A willingness to talk through the issues** coupled with **a dogged determination not to give up** eventually ensured the campaign was taken seriously.

## Approaching management

**1.** Removing pin-ups from areas used by manual workers high-lighted their continued presence within the white-collar areas of the DLO. In response to membership demands to pursue this issue, the item of pin-ups was placed on the agenda of the **normal monthly joint union/management meeting**; a formal complaint was also lodged about one office with the worst pictures. Union policy was to seek agreement with management for:

- a policy statement requiring all pin-ups to be removed from the offices within the DLO;
- management to send back the next consignment of calendars to the individual suppliers with a covering letter pointing out the reasons for their return and requesting calendars with alternative non-sexist pictures.

**2.** Management's initial reaction was to treat the agenda item as a joke. As men, manual workers were not expected to find the material offensive. Union arguments hinged around **the support already shown** by their members for the campaign, and the council's policy as an **equal opportunities employer**, a policy which they had done little to carry out. Pressure from the union for the topic to be treated as a genuine issue for discussion and negotiation sent management to the legal department for definitions of obscenity. The union side refused to be drawn on definitions of acceptable and unacceptable pin-ups, arguing that all offensive material should be withdrawn. Following management's refusal to move beyond the position of leaving it up to individuals, the union registered a **failure to agree** under the grievance procedure. By taking this action, the joint union committee indicated to management, as well as their own members, how seriously they were taking the issue.

**3.** Under the **next stage** of the grievance procedure, the issue was referred to the joint consultative committee, where unions negotiate with elected councillors. Once again, they were accused of time-wasting and pursuing trivial matters to the detriment of real workplace issues. Following a heated debate, in which the union side stressed again the council's responsibility as an equal opportunity employer and reminded councillors of Labour Party policy on equality for women, the elected members agreed to support the removal of pin-ups, but refused to insist that they be taken down. The unions were free to use persuasion but no more.

## Direct action

The union negotiating committee recognised that little more could be gained by taking the issue further through normal negotiating channels. If local management, who were by now well-versed in the arguments, would not act, there was little hope of convincing a negotiating structure outside and unconnected with the workplace. A **shift in tactics** towards direct action might prove more effective.

1. Senior stewards from the manual unions **refused to enter** the office where one wall was completely covered with particularly offensive pictures. As it was necessary to pass through this room in order to attend meetings with management, the daily work of the DLO suffered some disruption. Almost immediately, the offending material was removed.

2. A campaign of **retaliation** was proposed using photocopies of young, muscular male nudes, fully exposed. The manual union stewards encouraged women working in the offices to pin them up; where they feared victimisation, the stewards did it themselves. Male workers reacted with shock, ordering the women to take down the pictures. They refused to do so, unless the female pin-ups also came down. Challenged as to their hypocrisy, the men were unable to argue why the male pictures were more offensive than those of women. One consequence of this furore was to increase the interest in the campaign from women in the offices. The efforts exerted to keep the female pin-ups began to show how the pictures were an important part of some men's lives; it convinced those women who had previously considered the campaign a joke that many men did seriously regard women as sex-objects. Pursuing the campaign further needed union organisation within the offices to build on this increased awareness. The manual unions could do little more than informally encourage the action. Such support was not forthcoming and the issue began to fade.

## Impact of the campaign

Within the manual unions, the campaign has continued for more than two years and is still going on. Trade-union action to achieve a defined goal, such as a pay increase, is limited in duration; issues which challenge members' attitudes and behaviour need **constant reinforcement**. Little in the world outside work encourages men to maintain the campaign. Workplace action is undermined by newspapers and magazines selling the message of women as sex-objects. New workers join the sites, stewards stand down for someone else, and a few pin-ups reappear; as a result, discussion starts over again. But maintaining a workplace free of pin-ups is not the only outcome of the campaign. Shifting the attitudes of a predominantly male workforce towards greater respect for and understanding of women's position at work has led to a number of other developments. While none is spectacular, each represents a small step forward for women workers.

**1.** More women manual workers take an interest in union affairs. Prior to the campaign, mass site meetings of around 400 workers might include one woman; today a much larger number attend regularly. Outside the DLO, other women council employees have become aware of union activities.

**2.** Women white-collar staff are less willing to accept their inferior status within the offices, taking a more assertive stand on some issues. Manual union stewards complained informally to management about the sexual harassment. However, further action by women in the section was hampered by weak union organisation.

**3.** After union pressure, the council's recruitment programme for schools has been reorganised so that girls and boys receive the same information about job opportunities. Previously, when visiting schools, the training officer would talk separately to the boys about manual work and apprenticeship schemes, and then tell the girls about clerical work.

**4.** Young women have been taken on as apprentices in the DLO, the majority as painters and decorators. The first recruits had a rough time. The local paper 'congratulated' the council on its progressive policy by photographing the two women being manhandled by senior managers. The union demanded an apology from management for the humiliation suffered by the women because the picture stressed their sex rather than their role as workers. Later, there was an attempt to move one of the apprentices on to office work within the terms of her apprenticeship. She did not want to move and the union pursued the matter, pointing out that she would not receive sufficient training as a painter and decorator to get a job when her apprenticeship ended. She returned to painting and won the Apprentice of the Year award.

**5.** By refusing to accept that men, any more than women, should work in dirty, dangerous conditions, the unions are looking to campaign for better welfare facilities and more lifting equipment. They want rest areas on the sites to be cleaner and pleasanter and building materials packaged in smaller units.

**6.** Efforts are being made to tackle the language and behaviour of men towards women both in and out of work. Casual remarks about wives, girlfriends or women generally are picked up by stewards and talked through informally.

## Summary

The development of any union campaign is determined by the working environment of the participants. In this instance the predominantly male workforce had already built a strong trade-union organisation with experience of campaigning on a broad range of issues. As a result they could push their action against pin-ups further and faster than may be possible elsewhere. Nevertheless the success of their action is encouraging and may give other workplace committees ideas for future activity.

Where unions have difficulty in organising a co-ordinated campaign, workers should not be deterred from making smaller-scale protests. The press has reported a number of instances where women have taken action against degrading images of the female body displayed in their workplace.

■ **Example:** Women employees at Birmingham Social Services asked their shop steward to demand withdrawal of a poster advertising beds made by the department's industrial centre for the blind. The poster showed a négligé-clad blonde on one of the beds, inviting the public to 'Join me in a Woodville' bed.

■ **Example:** A council meeting in the London Borough of Lewisham discussed the problem of pin-ups in council buildings. This followed a complaint from the Women's Rights Working Party (a group of local councillors and women from community organisations) who had been asked to take the matter up on behalf of a woman employee. She had protested about pin-ups in her office by displaying a picture of a naked man, but she was ordered to take it down immediately. As a result of her complaint, the pin-ups were taken down in the town hall. (*New Statesman*, 7 December 1979.)

The press rarely treat such protests seriously. The Lewisham campaign prompted headlines such as 'Naughty nudes will be top of the agenda at council meeting tonight' (*Express*), 'Sexy pin-ups have town hall in a tizzy' (*Sun*), 'Boobs are busting out all over' (*Mirror*), 'A storm in a D-cup' (*Evening News*). Wherever possible, unions need to try and combat this trivialisation by issuing their own press releases and building a campaign around the initial protest.

The Sandwell campaign, and the protests mentioned above, show that women workers can succeed in getting pin-ups removed from their workplace. Taking action needs careful planning.

**1. Before launching a campaign**, make sure you have a **group of members** who are convinced the issue is worth pursuing. Individual action is difficult to sustain and leaves you open to victimisation. Unless the union is prepared to support the removal of pin-ups little may happen beyond a few token gestures. If the union is not interested, it may be necessary for a group of women members to start a campaign and convince the union of the seriousness of the issue as the campaign gains momentum.

**2. Spend plenty of time discussing** the issue with members before adopting a formal branch or workplace policy. **Regularly review the campaign** at committee meetings, assessing its strengths and weaknesses so far. Make sure union reps under attack from members are adequately supported by the rest of the committee.

**3. Link the campaign to union equal opportunities policies** and members' conditions of work. Avoid taking a moralistic approach likely to alienate members. The campaign needs to be seen as a union issue, not as a personal crusade.

**4. Examine ways of taking the issue up** with management using their equal opportunities policy or under the umbrella of working conditions. If there is sufficient membership support, use **formal procedures** as a way of indicating the seriousness of the issue.

**5. Consider appropriate industrial action** such as refusal to work in certain areas, or retaliation.

**6. Ensure other workplace issues are not neglected** as a result of the campaign. As it develops, look for ways of **broadening the issues** to take in other aspects of women's employment.

**7. Finally, be persistent** and do not give up after the first rebuff. Only by returning to the issue time and again is it likely to make a major impact on attitudes and behaviour in the workplace.

# Workplace questionnaires

During 1981 and 1982, workers in two local authorities, Camden (London) and Liverpool, undertook workplace surveys on sexism and sexual harassment. In both instances, the questionnaires were organised by NALGO, which represents white-collar council workers. Liverpool NALGO has around 5,100 members; Camden NALGO 3,700. The pattern of branch membership is similar to that of NALGO nationally (see p. 29), with women mainly employed in clerical and lower-grade administrative jobs, more senior posts being taken by men. Both branches operate a stewards' system within each department of the council – architects, social services, finance, housing, libraries, engineers.

Campaigning on sexual harassment at work was taken up by the equal opportunities committees of both branches. In Camden the initiative followed the concern of some women members at the way NALGO handled the case in Brent (see p. 78); Liverpool was one of the first branches to take up the issue as part of the activity within NALGO nationally to make sexual harassment a trade-union issue. Both branches decided to tackle the campaign by circulating a workplace questionnaire to members. Their experiences in organising the survey provide useful guidelines for others interested in taking up the idea.

### Why do a questionnaire?

Sort out your reasons for undertaking a questionnaire survey. Its purpose can be to:

- **obtain information** from members about incidents of sexual harassment and their attitudes to sexist behaviour in your workplace;
- **make members aware** of sexism and sexual harassment as a trade-union issue.

While these aims are not contradictory, a decision to emphasise one rather than the other may affect the content of the survey. Questions seeking information need to be precise and unambiguous; a broader range of questions can be included if the aim is to raise members' awareness. Although few will be returned if the questionnaire is too long, members are more likely to talk about the issues if they receive specific questions directed to them personally rather than being handed a general leaflet. The Camden and Liverpool surveys aimed at both; branches wanted to find out whether or not sexual harassment was a problem and how members saw the union dealing with complaints. At the same time, the consciousness-raising function of the questionnaire was important even for those members who chose not to return it.

Even where the main purpose of a questionnaire is to collect information, avoid promoting the survey as a scientific exercise. **There is no way it will prove exactly how much harassment occurs in your workplace.** A proportion of members may decide not to complete the questionnaire because they think it is 'silly', too personal, or too threatening. Others may misunderstand questions or deliberately spoil their answers. The branch may not be able to circulate all the members. The survey is valuable if it identifies *any* instances of harassment and encourages members to talk about the role of trade unions in combating sexism.

### Resources for the survey

Sort out how much **money, time and effort** the branch can afford to put into the questionnaire.

**1. Finance** will affect **the length and coverage of the survey**. In both Liverpool and Camden, the union branches paid for typing and printing – 750 four-page questionnaires in Liverpool, over 3,000 seven-page questionnaires in Camden. You will need to include the **costs of publicity, and envelopes** for members to return questionnaires in confidence. If you decide to collate the survey results using a computer, you may have to pay for **computer time**. An initial print-out of results for the Camden survey took about half-an-hour's computer time. Consider negotiating financial support from management using your trade-union facilities agreement. You could link this to discussions with management about a workplace policy for sexual harassment (see chapter 6).

**2.** Surveys are **time-consuming**. The survey period in Liverpool lasted several months, in Camden more than a year. Questions need careful discussion and piloting; survey sheets must be produced, distributed and collected; the results collated and analysed. As unions gain more experience of useful questions, some of these procedures will speed up.

It also depends on how many people are available to organise the survey. In both workplaces, the equal opportunities committees, a core of about six people, administered the questionnaire, drawing on the support of stewards and activists from time to time. In Liverpool 179 survey returns were analysed manually; Camden's 970 returns were coded for computer analysis. The larger the survey, the more useful a computer. Results can be presented by department or according to the respondent's age/ sex/grade of job. **Only use a computer if the union can call on experienced operators for advice before drawing up the question- naire.** You can organise a worthwhile survey without access to a computer. Computers cannot easily cope with members' com- ments and queries. Time used in coding and punching data may be better spent sorting out the information by hand. Members who are hesitant about taking on the political aspects of union work may welcome an opportunity to contribute to the mechani- cal tasks involved in organising the survey.

## Coverage

Decide on what proportion of the membership you want to include in the survey. Your choices are to:

- include both men and women, or survey women members only;
- cover the whole workplace or only particular sections/ departments;
- include all members or only a selected sample.

**1.** Making this decision depends partly on the **resources** avail- able to organise the questionnaire and on the **size** of the member- ship. In a workplace with less than 500 members, it is feasible to circulate everyone. With greater numbers you may prefer to select certain sections as more likely to have problems or where more women are employed. However, if departments are small, members may be reluctant to complete the questionnaire for fear of easy identification. On the other hand, tackling a workforce of several thousand is a daunting task; it may be helpful to stagger the circulation over several months, sending a new batch out as the previous group is returned. Results could be collated as you go along, but not released until the survey was complete.

Camden chose to survey the entire membership of over 3,000 on the grounds that a major purpose of the questionnaire was to raise members' awareness of the issues. In Liverpool, limited resources restricted circulation to 750 women members out of a female membership of about 2,800. The number of question- naires allocated to a department depended on its size; stewards then handed questionnaires to as many women members as possible, making sure they went first to any women who expressed an interest in filling it in.

2. Whether or not to include men in the questionnaire should be debated within the union. You may decide, as Liverpool NALGO did, that sexual harassment is overwhelmingly **a problem for women** and their needs should be the branch's first concern. As men are rarely victims of harassment, many of the questions would be inappropriate. Some men would not take the issue seriously and distort the survey results by spoiling their answers. You could make the questionnaire available to any man who specifically requested to fill one in; this happened in Liverpool. Alternatively, you may decide the **whole membership** should be involved. Camden divided their questionnaire into three parts – an introductory section on sexism generally for all members; a section for women on their experiences of sexual harassment; and a section for men dealing with their attitudes towards women. A large number of men completed the questionnaire. However, questions about male attitudes towards women do assume all men are heterosexual; a questionnaire designed for the whole membership may need a separate section to cover the experiences of gay male workers.

## Sorting out the questions

1. The **content of the questionnaire** will depend on the aims of the survey. Decide whether or not you want to find out about a range of sexist practices or only about incidents of sexual harassment. Camden took the former approach, asking about attitudes to women's jobs, domestic responsibilities, rights to time off to look after sick children and the need for part-time work following maternity leave. The Liverpool survey was more restricted, concentrating on sexual harassment, attitudes to women, and pin-ups. To sort out the content, **start by jotting down everything you want to know**, for example:

- who has experienced harassment;
- what sort of harassment;
- what they did about it.

Talk through all the points, identifying those which are **essential** for the survey to be of use. The longer the questionnaire, the less likely members are to fill it in and the more complex the analysis of the results.

**2.** Turn each of the points into questions which only require members to tick a particular answer. You may need several questions to cover one point. Put the questions into logical sequence. Be wary of including too many open questions where members are asked to comment. While it seems attractive to let members develop their own ideas, such questions are almost impossible to analyse. Predetermined questions, while limiting the range of possible answers, are much easier to handle. You can give members a chance to add their own comments at the end.

**3.** The questions must be clear and unambiguous. Check they will be understood by trying them out on a sample of members **unfamiliar** with the issues. It is easy for the compiler of a questionnaire to assume people know more about the topic than they do. Most trade unionists will have thought little about sexism so questions should spell out details of what is involved. Here is one example of a question aimed at finding out members' attitudes to sexual harassment:

■ Do you think sexual harassment at work reflects the inferior position of women in the workplace?

Yes/No

This is a bad question because it assumes the respondent accepts that women are disadvantaged at work. When collating the answers it would be difficult to decide whether a 'no' answer meant 'sexual harassment is not one of the ways women experience inferiority at work' or 'women are not inferior at work'. Far better to ask a more straightforward question about how members feel about sexual harassment and use the results of the questionnaire to illustrate how harassment reinforces discrimination against women.

**4.** To give you some ideas the handbook includes a set of **basic questions** compiled from various sexual harassment questionnaires, including those used by Camden and Liverpool NALGO. These are shown on pp. 112–16. They should be used as a resource-bank from which you can select questions relevant to your own needs. The questions cover definitions of sexual harassment, attitudes to and responses to harassment, and background information about the workplace. The section on sexism is confined to those aspects most closely associated with harassment. A questionnaire such as this would be aimed at women members. Other questions should be included if the union wants to involve the whole membership.

5. Once the questionnaire is complete, decide on a suitable **title**. Members may be less responsive to a survey about 'sexism' than one promoted as dealing with 'equal opportunities'. You will need a short **covering letter** introducing the questionnaire; some members may have missed the publicity or forgotten about it. Liverpool NALGO introduced their questionnaire as follows:

> Sexual harassment at work is an issue which affects all women and recently gained some publicity, and whose prevalence is at present being researched by NALGO nationally. We do not feel this is an issue which can be dismissed by saying that women enjoy attention or bring it on themselves. Neither do we feel that it can be overlooked by us as one of the hazards of women's employment. We as a branch, through the Equal Opportunities Committeee must first investigate the prevalence of sexual harassment among our members and secondly through discussion and consultation, seek ways of dealing with the problem as it exists and ultimately its cessation.
>
> We would therefore appreciate your co-operation in completing the attached questionnaire and any comments you may have on the matter.
>
> Any cases of sexual harassment may be taken up with your shop steward and will be treated in the strictest confidence.

### A selection of questions on sexual harassment and sexism at work

#### A. *Work situation*
1. Grade/Job ............     2. Dept./Section ..........
3. During a normal working day, do you come into contact with:
   - mainly women
   - mainly men
   - roughly equal numbers of both

4. Is your immediate supervisor:
   - a man
   - a woman

#### B. *Sexual harassment*
1. Which of the following statements best reflects the way you feel?

- Innocent flirtation at work is just a bit of fun
- A woman has to expect unpleasant sexual advances and learn to put up with them
- Unwelcome attention from men at work is offensive
- Women who are bothered by men at work are usually 'asking for it'

2. (i) While at work, have you ever had any unwanted sexual remarks, looks, suggestions, or physical contact from men that causes you discomfort?

- Yes
- No

(ii) If yes, were these:

- in your present job
- in your previous job

(iii) If in your present job, were these:

- being presented with offensive material, e.g. pin-ups
- being stared and leered at
- sexual remarks or teasing
- touching, brushing against, grabbing
- propositions of love-making
- other more serious sexual assault

(iv) If in your previous job, was this a reason for your leaving that job?

- Yes
- No

3. Who sexually harassed you?

- The supervisor
- Management other than the supervisor
- Co-worker
- Patient/customer/client

4. Which of the following statements most closely describes your reactions to harassment (tick more than one if appropriate)?

- Didn't affect you at all
- Felt embarrassed
- Felt angry

- Felt flattered
- Felt guilty
- Felt put in your place
- Made you ill (e.g. upset stomach, nerves, headache, etc.)

5. Have any incidents of sexual harassment affected your work situation in any way, by:

- making you less friendly
- making you dress differently
- making you avoid the man/men
- making you lose interest in your work
- spoiling your chances of promotion
- affecting your job performance
- making you consider leaving or asking for a transfer
- other (specify if possible)

6. What responses have you made to incidents of sexual harassment? (Tick as many as are appropriate)

- None, ignored it
- Played along for the sake of peace and quiet
- Given as good as you got
- Told the man to stop
- Reported it to the union
- Reported it to management
- Discussed it with people you work with
- Discussed it with people outside work
- Taken days off work
- Asked for a transfer

7. If you have reported any incidents of sexual harassment, was it:

- taken seriously and dealt with effectively
- dealt with seriously at the time, but recurred since
- not taken seriously and nothing done about it
- dealt with by blaming you in some way (please specify)

8. If you have not reported the incident(s), please indicate your reasons.

. . . . . . . . . . . . . . . . . . . . . . . . . . . . . . . . . . . . . . . . . . . . . . . . . . .
. . . . . . . . . . . . . . . . . . . . . . . . . . . . . . . . . . . . . . . . . . . . . . . . . . .
. . . . . . . . . . . . . . . . . . . . . . . . . . . . . . . . . . . . . . . . . . . . . . . . . . .

9. How would you like the union to take up cases of sexual harassment? (Tick more than one if appropriate)

- By keeping the issue within the union
- By dealing with it through normal union/management procedures
- By referring it straight to management
- By appointing a woman union officer to take up complaints

10. If you have any other comments, please list them below.

## C. Sexism

1. Do you think a woman's physical attractiveness is important in:

- getting her a job
- keeping her in the job
- getting promotion
- being offered more interesting work

2. Do you sometimes feel that the recognition you are given at work is partly due to your physical attractiveness rather than your work skills?

- Yes
- No

3. Many of the jobs in this workplace traditionally done by women are low-paid, (e.g. (give example)). Do you think this is because:

- these jobs are unskilled and therefore low-paid
- these jobs are skilled, but the skills involved are not recognised
- these jobs are undervalued because they are done by women (e.g. if typing were a male craft job, it would be more highly paid)
- other

4. (i) In your workplace, are there pictures of naked/semi-naked women or other material of a sexually-explicit nature?

- Yes
- No

(ii) If yes, do you find these pictures:

- flattering to women
- just a bit of fun
- embarrassing
- insulting and should be removed
- so commonplace you hardly notice them

5. Do you consider the following terms derogatory when applied to an adult woman while she is working?

- 'girl'                              *yes*          *no*
- 'luv'
- 'gorgeous'
- 'sexy'
- 'dear'

6. Do you sometimes feel you are treated in a condescending manner at work by:

- male co-workers                    *yes*          *no*
- male supervisors
- female co-workers
- female supervisors

## Preparing for the survey

The success of the survey depends on detailed preparation before it is distributed.

**1.** The branch/workplace committee should **formally approve** the campaign if it is to carry any weight with members. Make sure union officers and stewards understand the issues; even if they have not been involved in the initial preparation, their co-operation is needed for distributing questionnaires and encouraging members to participate. **It is worth spending time going over the arguments about trade-union approaches to sexual harassment.** Stewards will be deluged with questions and comments when the questionnaire reaches their section. In both examples, the departments returning the least number of questionnaires were those where stewards remained unconvinced of the need for the survey. If male stewards are reluctant to participate, either through embarrassment or a feeling that the issue should be tackled by women, **arrange for women activists to take on responsibility** for that particular section. In Liverpool, the question aire was distributed by both stewards and members of the equal opportunities committee.

**2.** Members need to know about the survey **well in advance**. Few will respond favourably to being suddenly confronted with a questionnaire about an issue which may be seen as private and personal. Start to build interest in the questionnaire through **ublicity leaflets, workplace meetings and report-backs** from nion committees. At the outset, members may well not accept that sexual harassment is a problem in your workplace or a egitimate issue for the union to pursue. You may be accused of wasting time and money. As harassment is a taken-for-granted art of working life, women experiencing it may not recognise the behaviour of male co-workers or superiors as such. **Informal iscussions** at lunchtime or breaks, using examples from similar workplaces, will make members more aware of sexist practices. If possible **arrange a union meeting with an outside speaker or a film** a few weeks before the questionnaire is circulated (see the nd of this chapter for more details). When the questionnaire is ready, ask stewards to **organise section meetings** where the details of the questionnaire can be explained before members fill it in.

**3.** You may want to prepare a **press statement** about the urvey. Local papers are quick to pick up unusual events, particularly if they appear to involve sex. Liverpool branch was nundated with press enquiries once their questionnaire had een distributed. Local radio and television also picked up the ory. If the press catch you unprepared, you may regret your ff-the-cuff answers to their, no doubt, mischievous questions. A ress release may encourage a paper to present the story from the union's point of view. The statement should cover:

- why sexual harassment is a trade-union issue;
- why your branch/workplace decided to undertake a survey;
- brief details of the survey;
- any results of the survey.

eep the statement short, around 300 words, and be ready to nswer questions on it. The Pluto Handbook *Using the Media* gives formation on dealing with the press. Not all workplaces will be pproached by the media. If you are left alone, it is wiser not to ek publicity on this issue. Newspapers rarely treat sexual harass-ent seriously. Stories about the recently published NCCL pam-let appeared under headlines shouting 'Office Lotharios feel the nch', 'Hands off the office wolf', and 'It's war on the office pests'.

**4.** Decide whether or not you need to **inform managemen** about the survey. Neither Camden nor Liverpool did so, sinc the issue was internal to the union. Despite the subsequer publicity in Liverpool, management there maintained a low pr file. If you think your management might ask questions, prepar a response in advance. They may be concerned that the que tionnaire is aimed at them or is disrupting the workforce. A though initially a union matter, you may need to approach ther later to take up a complaint of harassment or negotiate a ne grievance procedure.

### Distribution, collection and analysis

**1.** Once the questionnaire is ready, distribute it through th branch. Give members reasonable time to fill it in, perhaps tw weeks; then send out a **reminder** setting a deadline for replie Ask stewards to go round encouraging members to fill them in.

**2.** Remember to include an envelope with the questionnai so that members can **reply in confidence**. Few will be completed members think someone in the section has access to their replie Depending on how your workplace is organised, you can as stewards to collect sealed envelopes, have them sent through th internal mail, or place a collection box at a convenient location

**3.** Once you think most of the replies have been returned start sorting out the results. Check first which sections and grade have returned most/least replies; if necessary make enquirie about poor returns.

**4.** Even if the analysis takes some time, try to **publicise** pr liminary results quickly. This will help maintain interest in th issue and lay the groundwork for any action the branch may wa to take to follow up the questionnaire. Make the issue a regul item on branch or shop steward committee agendas; produce poster highlighting the key results for the union notice-boar include a brief summary in the union newsletter. The prelimina reports for both Camden and Liverpool NALGO showed men bers that sexual harassment was a serious problem in bo workplaces.

### Report of Liverpool NALGO Equal Opportunities Workin Party questionnaire on sexual harassment

A total of 750 questionnaires were distributed to a variety ( departments by the stewards or staff committee. Women in wide range of departments, jobs and grades were reached. Of the total returned to the branch office:

- 183 questionnaires were returned of which six were spoiled;
- 98 women had experienced sexual harassment of whom 55 were harassed at their present workplace;
- 27 women were harassed by being stared or leered at or by receiving sexual remarks;
- 26 were harassed by being touched, brushed against or grabbed;
- only five of the women had reported the harassment and of those, two found their complaint taken seriously.

Thus over 50 per cent of women who replied had experienced sexual harassment at some time and over 25 per cent reported it happening in their present workplace. Additional questions gave information that the majority of women harassed felt either embarrassed or angry, although the majority reacted by adopting a 'cool, guarded manner' or had to 'pretend not to notice'. The number of cases of harassment, therefore, validates our original belief that sexual harassment exists at work and should be taken seriously by trade unions. While it may appear a limited return, nevertheless, we feel that 25 per cent of women reporting sexual harassment in their current workplace is a significant figure, particularly if this is multiplied across the authority.

### Report of Camden NALGO questionnaire in branch newsletter

There were a total of 970 questionnaires returned unspoilt, of which 441 were completed by men and 514 by women.

#### Participation in the workforce

A significant number of those who filled out the questionnaire felt that women were considered a disadvantage by employers when being considered for promotion. Most people, however, felt that women were as capable as men of doing the job. A majority of respondents felt that women in low-paid jobs have their skills unrecognised and undervalued. Men were almost equally divided in thinking that calling women 'girls' was derogatory. More than half the women answering felt that it was. There were 680 members who felt that people should have paid time off to look after sick dependants, a majority of them men. This is a clear mandate for branch action.

## Sexual harassment

When asked for an opinion on pictures of naked women o
view in offices, 524 members (319 women, 205 men) felt tha
they were degrading to women and should be removed. A
number of people complained of sexual harassment from
members of the public but not from colleagues; and 7 men an
4 women felt that sexual harassment happens to men too. O
the question of how the union should deal with sexual harass
ment at work, most women felt there should be a woma
union official to whom they could go and talk. Many peopl
felt constrained by the questions. Some felt they wanted to g
beyond the Yes/No answer allowed, and some felt the ques
tions did not allow for the answers they wanted to give. Ther
were 24 men and 12 women who felt the questionnaire a wast
of time and money; 64 people specifically welcomed it eve
though many thought it was only a start.

## Impact of the questionnaire on the workplace

How unions respond to the results of a survey depends on th
information received and the attitudes of members to the issue
raised. For both Liverpool and Camden NALGO the question
naire fulfilled its aim of developing members' awareness of sexis
practices, including sexual harassment. Despite the uneve
response between different sections of their workplaces an
some overt hostility from a minority of members, the membe
ship generally saw the activity as worthwhile. As a result, bot
branches have found that the survey generated a number c
union and workplace initiatives, all of which are helping to buil
understanding about women's position at work.

**1.** Prior to the survey, both equal opportunities committee
had received little publicity within the branch. By organising th
questionnaire, members became aware of the committee's exis
tence. Equal opportunities work is taken more seriously an
members now receive regular information about committe
business. More items about women are appearing in branc
newsletters. This has been important not only in ensuring tha
the union moves forward on the issue of harassment but also i
bringing other equal opportunities issues to the union's attention

**2.** Incidents of sexual harassment recorded by member
clearly established the need for trade-union action to deal wit
complaints. Since the survey, both branches have taken up com

plaints referred by members, not all of which resulted in formal approaches to management. Often, women wanted only to talk about their problem with someone sympathetic. The issue is no longer greeted with sniggers but accepted by many members as a serious issue for women at work.

3. By encouraging women to come forward with complaints, the survey highlighted previous inadequacies for women in the union's organisation. Members recommended women union officers be appointed to take up complaints of harassment; clearly women felt male stewards were not always best suited to tackle their problems.

4. Both branches are looking at their policy and procedures on equal opportunities. Camden have adopted an equal opportunities policy for the branch and are taking the issue up with management. Liverpool have drafted a special grievance procedure for taking up complaints of sexual harassment.

5. The surveys revealed the need for union training on sexism and sexual harassment. So far, Liverpool have introduced the issue into equal opportunities and women's training schools. Case studies on sexual harassment are included in grievance-handling training for shop stewards and branch officers.

6. As well as sexual harassment, the surveys identified other issues for union action. Camden are pursuing members' demands for paid time off to look after sick children; their survey also revealed considerable interest in facilities for women to work part-time following maternity leave. Since the survey, Liverpool have started negotiating child-care facilities, opportunities for job-sharing, and for cervical smear tests to be available to women at the workplace.

7. Women have begun to take a more active interest in the union. Camden now have women on their branch executive; Liverpool always include women on their negotiating team to meet management. There are also training courses for women members interested in becoming shop stewards. Male union activists are more careful about using sexist language and overt sexist behaviour at union meetings has declined considerably.

## Summary

As with the Sandwell pin-ups campaign, the detailed operation of the questionnaire in both examples was determined by local conditions. Both surveys were undertaken by branches whose large memberships are located in a number of buildings within their localities. The resulting problems for the organising group in maintaining close contact with the membership throughout the campaign contributed to some extent to the low rate of return from a few sections. Counter to this, the familiarity with form-filling associated with white-collar work in local authorities meant members had little difficulty in understanding and completing the questionnaire. At the same time, branches had equal opportunities committees involving members with interest and experience in the women's movement. Since the union was already taking up women's issues, tackling a questionnaire on sexual harassment became part of their on-going work.

Branches without any history of campaigning on women's issues need to consider carefully the most appropriate way of developing union action on sexual harassment. Rather than start with a workplace questionnaire, it would perhaps be more useful in the first instance to encourage women union activists to meet together as a women's group or equal opportunities committee. Shop stewards committees should ensure that regular discussions and report-back to members take place about the working conditions of their women members, such as child-care, maternity leave, time off for sick dependants, etc. As members become aware of the specific needs of working women, the issue of sexual harassment at work can be raised formally. As the examples show, a survey is no substitute for informal discussions about sexism and sexual harassment. Small workplaces may find such discussions sufficient to identify problems for union action. However, even in the most friendly working environment, women may be afraid to speak out about sexist behaviour. By turning individual complaints into an examination of equal opportunities in working conditions, a confidential questionnaire ensures that sexual harassment is regarded as a trade-union issue.

## Meetings

Any campaign involves unions organising meetings with members. Most branches find difficulty in attracting members to meetings outside work time and few members attend unless the agenda is relevant to their particular problems. In some instances, the content and format of union meetings is changing so as to encourage membership involvement. Any meeting to discuss sexism and sexual harassment at work should be planned carefully. Few members are familiar with the issue or willing to talk openly about their feelings; many may be embarrassed by references to sexual propositions. To be successful, the meeting must overcome fears and create an environment in which sexist behaviour can be discussed openly and honestly. The following points may help in organising such a meeting.

## Purpose of the meeting

A discussion on sexism and sexual harassment could cover a range of issues or concentrate on one specific aspect. Rather than cram everything into a single session, you may find it more satisfactory to give people time to think and talk by arranging a series of meetings to cover:

- **information to members** about what constitutes sexual harassment, the impact and consequences of harassment on women workers, why harassment is a trade-union issue;
- **members' experiences of sexual harassment** and sexist behaviour in the workplace;
- **union policies on sexual harassment** such as the TUC guidelines etc., procedures for handling members' complaints;
- possible **workplace action to combat sexism and sexual harassment**, such as a pin-up campaign, questionnaire, negotiating a workplace policy.

## The participants

Decide whether or not you want the meeting to be women-only or mixed. Mixed meetings have the advantage of encouraging men to take the issue seriously. Any decision about union policy or workplace action needs the support of the whole membership. However, women members must have some opportunity to meet together without men to talk about their experiences of harassment. Women-only meetings enable members to speak without fear of ridicule or challenge by male members. Women can talk about specific incidents of harassment knowing the harasser is not present. You could, therefore, consider starting with a general information meeting for everyone, following this up with women-only meetings. Unions which have tried this approach found the mixed meeting attracted few women, who remained quiet during the discussion. However, at their own meeting women spoke about instances of harassment and their reaction to sexist behaviour. You might prefer to hold the women-only meeting first, so that women members could sort out their ideas and present them to a mixed meeting; that way no one would be talking just about themselves.

## Time of meetings

Finding an appropriate time for meetings is a continuing problem for all unions. For many women, time outside work is taken up by shopping, cooking and looking after children. Ideally, meetings should be held in working time so that everyone can attend. Sexual harassment is an aspect of members' working conditions so it should be possible to arrange section meetings to deal with issues of union/management policy. However, members as well as management may query the use of working time for meetings with a film or outside speaker aimed at raising general awareness of sexism. You may prefer to start by having a few meetings out of work hours, timed as conveniently as possible for women members; once sufficient interest is shown in the issue, subsequent meetings could be held in working time. Alternatively, you may want to think about negotiating time as part of a union/management training programme on sexual harassment.

## Content of meeting

Starting a discussion about a new topic is often helped by inviting an outside speaker or using a film. Both approaches may be useful for an introductory meeting about sexual harassment. Someone who appears knowledgeable about a topic and is experienced at dealing with sensitive questions can create a positive atmosphere for subsequent discussion. An increasing number of unions are developing national policies on sexual harassment and should have names of suitable speakers; for information, contact your union department with responsibility for women or health and safety at work.

There are two videos available for hire dealing with sexual harassment at work, although neither is based on British examples. *It's Just a Compliment, Luv* is an Australian film about the experiences of women working in the postal industry. It highlights their feelings, the different types of behaviour women experience as harassment, and the role of unions in organising to resist sexual harassment. The second, *It's Not Your Imagination*, made in Canada, explores the views of five women who have been sexually harassed at work. Two women union reps give their definition of harassment and discuss the obligation of unions to protect their members. Although the details of each film refer to their respective countries, they raise general issues which may help convince members that sexual harassment is a serious workplace problem. Both films run for about 25 minutes and can be hired from Cinema of Women (address at the end of the book). A video examining union approaches to harassment in this country is planned and should hopefully be available in the near future.

If you decide not to use a film or outside speaker, explore other ways of making the issue relevant to your members. You may want to produce a fact sheet using some of the statistics from this handbook, or to illustrate your opening remarks with examples from workplaces similar to your own. As most people will start by arguing that sexual harassment is a personal problem, remember to link the discussion to women's position at work.

## Format of the meeting

The meeting will be more successful if you think about ways of encouraging members to participate. Most people are intimidated in large meetings where they sit in rows staring at someone else's back, and looking up at a platform. Reorganising the furniture into a circle or semi-circle will help everyone see who is at the meeting and feel part of the group. People are more likely to discuss sensitive issues if they can talk in small groups of four or five rather than in a meeting of 50 or 500. You might consider arranging an introductory meeting on sexual harassment as follows:

- participants start by sitting in a circle or semi-circle to see a film or listen to a speaker;
- break up into small groups for discussion, perhaps using a fact sheet or set of questions about trade-union approaches to sexual harassment (with a mixed group, you might like to try women/men-only small groups);
- return to large groups after 30 minutes for brief report-back from small groups and decisions about future meetings/activities.

## Publicity

Publicity is an essential part of any union campaign. Some branches/workplaces produce their own newsletters and leaflets, others circulate nationally produced materials. Following NALGO's national leaflet, other unions are producing their own material about sexual harassment at work. They are a useful introduction to the issues and branches should obtain enough copies for all their members. Local publicity material, however, often makes more impact with members since it can refer to familiar situations. To prepare your own publicity, think about the following points.

## Purpose of the leaflet/newsletter item

As with a meeting, you may want to give members general information about sexual harassment or deal with a specific aspect of the problem. Publicity material might cover:

- **information** to members about what constitutes sexual harassment and why it is a trade-union issue;
- **procedures and actions** available to members with complaints of sexual harassment;
- **union policies** at national/local level about sexual harassment at work;
- **advance information** of a meeting or workplace campaign about sexual harassment at work.

## Sorting out content

The purpose of the newsletter will determine what you put in it. Members will find the publicity useful and interesting if it includes **practical advice relevant to your workplace**. Try to ensure some of the following points are included in any item:

- **experiences and examples** of sexist behaviour/sexual harassment in your workplace (or one similar to your own);
- **definition** of what is/is not sexist behaviour/sexual harassment, together with arguments as to why sexism is a trade-union issue;
- **practical steps** which members can take to file a complaint or tackle sexism in your workplace;
- the name of a **contact** and/or information about a **meeting or workplace activity** connected with sexism and sexual harassment.

The two examples of a newsletter which follow include several of these points. They are specific to a workplace or occupation, present members with trade-union approaches to the issue, and one announces the start of a union campaign.

■ **Example:** *Don't be caught with . . . yours down*
  It's about time we started seriously to tackle sexism in Haringey NALGO. That means sexism among our own membership as

well as our employers. For example, a poster was recently brought to the attention of the Women's Subcommittee by a council member who found it in the gents toilet at the Civic Centre. It was displayed on a notice-board. The poster depicted a woman holding a clipboard and posing coyly. Her feet are bare, she wears a brief mini-skirt and she has a scanty pair of underpants halfway down her legs. Her expression says 'come and get me' as she sucks on a pen. The caption reads, 'Don't be caught with . . . yours down! Buy a Mayday Disco ticket now', and goes on to give details of an office party at Woodall House.

This poster conforms with the idealised image of women as sex-objects, the sexual fantasy available to any man. More than 50 per cent of NALGO members are women. Many of us are wives and mothers, and probably all of us are sexual beings. But we are union members because of our paid employment. Our lives are not limited to the roles which these pictures show. The Women's Subcommittee believes it is an insult to suggest that women's lives are in any way restricted. We recognise that many women enjoy being wives and mothers but this does not represent the totality of women's working lives as such images suggest. We believe it is an insult to turn any human being into an object to be leered at, to be used by others for their own fanciful gratification. (*Voiceprint*, Haringey NALGO.)

**Example:** *Learning to recognise sexual harassment at work*
All of us work with men and in male hierarchies, some of us have male groups of students – all of which can make our working lives very difficult.

Women in workplaces like ours and elsewhere are increasingly reporting instances of sexual harassment at work. This has to be seen as part of the degrading and discriminatory treatment of women workers in work situations that are class and gender divided.

Sexual harassment ranges from innuendo, dirty jokes, pin-ups, comments about clothes and looks, sexual overtures, touching, assault and rape. The strain of harassment and often the consequences of non-compliance can result in severe physical and mental damage. It is therefore an issue of our health and safety at work as well as our right to be treated as equals and not as powerless victims of male sexual oppression. In the

USA victims of sexual harassment are now able to receive compensation and in Britain at least one case of unfair dismissal over complaints of unwanted advances was upheld, but another taken up by NALGO women workers was lost – no doubt in part due to the union having to represent the offender. In fighting for women's rights at work it is necessary for unions to take this issue as an important one.

The Inner London Women's Rights Committee will be discussing this issue in the future. If anyone has any information or experiences they would like to give (it would be treated anonymously) we would be pleased to receive it. (Inner London NATFHE, *Newsletter*, 5.)

### Production and layout

Few members will read a scruffy, boring leaflet or newsletter. Unfortunately, some unions produced rather dull leaflets about sexual harassment for fear of overplaying the issue. To attract interest, information needs to be written in a lively style and illustrated if at all possible. How you do this depends to some extent on your production method – duplicator, photocopier or ptinting. In designing your leaflet/newsletter:

- keep your sentences short and simple, avoid jargon and **sexist language**;
- break up the text into **short paragraphs** with bold headings – these can either be drawn freehand or made using stencils, or you can buy special lettering;
- use pictures – a **sexist cartoon or photograph** can help illustrate your argument;
- lay out the information with **plenty of space** so it is easy to read and makes an attractive design – it is better to have too little material than so much everything is crammed together.

Below is an example of a simple leaflet for advertising a meeting.

■ **Example:**

---

### THE ABC UNION

---

SEXUAL HARASSMENT AT WORK IS:

- being stared and leered at
- receiving sexual comments and jokes
- being touched, brushed against or grabbed
- having offensive pin-ups in the workplace
- receiving unwanted demands for sex

SEXUAL HARASSMENT CAN CAUSE THE VICTIM:

- to leave her job
- to be transferred to less satisfactory work
- to lose a chance of promotion or training
- to suffer stress and sickness
- to work in unpleasant conditions

---

### EVERY WORKER HAS THE RIGHT TO A WORKPLACE FREE FROM SEXUAL HARASSMENT

---

To find out more about the problem and what the union can do to combat sexual harassment at work, come to a discussion meeting on

Monday 10 January 12 noon – 1 p.m. Room D

*Video:* 'It's just a compliment luv'

Coffee available – please bring lunch

---

# 6.

# Collective agreements

Negotiating arguments / management policies / training programmes / procedures for handling complaints.

Trade-union involvement in combating sexual harassment at work goes beyond campaigning to increase membership awareness of the problem. Unions exist to protect and improve the work situation of members through collective bargaining. A harassment-free workplace cannot be achieved **unless unions insist their employer takes the issue seriously**. Responsibility for running the workplace lies with management, who have a **duty to ensure safe and non-discriminatory working conditions** for all employees. Sexual harassment within the workplace reflects a lack of management interest about the working conditions of their women employees.

With the exception of a few employers in the public sector, employers in this country have not yet accepted sexual harassment as an issue for management action. Unions need to approach their management to negotiate a **workplace policy** which clearly identifies sexual harassment as an unacceptable and discriminatory practice. Unions may be able to tackle incidents of harassment between members without involving management, but complaints of harassment by a supervisor cannot easily be dealt with outside a formal procedure. When approached, management are unlikely to take up such complaints unless they are already aware of the consequences of sexual harassment both for the victim and for themselves. A **training programme for management** is as essential as developing awareness of the issues within the union.

This training programme should not only deal with the causes and consequences of sexual harassment but also provide a clear indication to managers and supervisors of how the union and management intend to take up complaints. Unions may need to **amend their grievance procedures** to make sure they adequately cover cases of discrimination and harassment. Using the normal negotiating channels for complaints of harassment emphasises to management the seriousness with which unions view the problem, and makes it clear that, as with any other workplace problem, an inability to resolve the complaint to the union's satisfaction may lead to industrial action.

The lack of concern about sexual harassment shown by British employers is not shared by their counterparts in the USA. Many of the larger employers rushed to produce company policies and procedures for dealing with cases of harassment following the publication of guidelines on sexual harassment by the Equal Employment Opportunities Commission (the US equivalent of the Equal Opportunities Commission in Britain). Unless employers have taken 'all necessary steps to prevent sexual harassment occurring', they may be financially liable under US discrimination laws for allowing an employee to be discriminated against by suffering sexual harassment. US courts have awarded sums of around $20,000 in compensation to victims of sexual harassment.

In Britain, under section 41(1) of the Sex Discrimination Act 1975, an **employer is responsible for the discriminatory acts of employees**, whether or not the employer was aware of the practice. The employer's liability is reduced only if 'reasonably practicable steps' have been taken to prevent discrimination. Unions may find it useful to argue that a negotiated workplace policy for dealing with sexual harassment would be one way their employer can show an intent to eradicate discrimination. Once it is firmly established that sexual harassment is a form of sex discrimination under the terms of the Sex Discrimination Act (see chapter 7), some employers may well be keen to introduce workplace policies so as to limit their liability. In such cases, unions need to ensure that procedures proposed by management pay more than lip-service to the problem and are backed up by a determination to put the procedures into practice. To forestall this situation, unions should begin now to formulate their own proposals for a workplace policy. This might include:

- **a statement on sexual harassment at work;**
- **a training programme about sexual harassment for management and employees;**
- **joint union/management procedures for dealing with cases of sexual harassment.**

# Negotiating arguments

Unions need to sort out their arguments before starting negotiations with management. Employers will resist demands for sexual harassment to be treated as a workplace issue requiring management action. Some claims that they may put forward are outlined below.

**1.** Sexual harassment is not a serious problem but a bit of fun between workers which helps to brighten up the routine. If management step in, workers will complain of their 'kill-joy' attitude and may cause trouble.

**2.** Sexual harassment is a personal matter between two people. Men are naturally attracted to women, who expect a few compliments. After all, workplace romances are commonplace, and management cannot intervene in employees' private lives.

**3.** Women who are constantly pestered by men at work ask for it by the way they walk or dress. Women who flirt cannot complain if it sometimes gets out of hand. They created the problem so they should be able to handle it themselves.

**4.** Sexual harassment might be a problem on the rare occasion. If it happens, current workplace procedures are adequate to deal with it so there is no need to issue a policy or start a training programme. If there is any difficulty, the welfare officer is competent to handle such problems.

To counter these points, unions should present a **well-prepared** case. **Membership support** for the negotiations is vital for their success, and unions would be wise to open negotiations only after some campaigning activity among members. Management attempts to laugh off union approaches will fall flat only if members are convinced that sexual harassment is a trade-union issue. It may also be worthwhile sounding out any members of management likely to be sympathetic. Women managers may themselves have been subjected to sexual harassment, or may at least have some understanding of the issues involved. Your negotiating arguments should include the following.

**1. Information** from surveys about the **incidence and nature** of harassment, supported if possible by examples from your own workplace. If not, present a range of possible situations using cases from a similar workplace. You need to get over the point that sexual harassment is a hidden but frequent part of working life for many women.

**2.** Sexual harassment creates **unsatisfactory working condi-**

**tions** and presents a **health and safety hazard** to women workers. Outline the stress and sickness consequences of harassment. Remind management of their responsibility under the Health and Safety at Work Act for the health, safety and welfare of their employees.

**3.** Sexual harassment may well be in breach of the **employer's responsibility** to provide equal opportunities for all employees under the Sex Discrimination Act. Women who experience harassment suffer a deterioration in their working conditions, may be refused training or promotion, or be unwilling to take advantage of new opportunities for fear of increasing harassment. To avoid their harasser, some women leave or seek a transfer, so reducing their chances of advancement. They gain an unfair reputation for being unreliable. Management need a policy which indicates their opposition to sexual harassment, so as to confirm their commitment to real equal opportunities in the workplace.

**4.** The employer **loses money** through sexual harassment because of the victim's absenteeism, poor work performance, transfer to other work or decision to leave. Her distress also affects co-workers. Refer to the US federal government survey which estimated losses of $189 million over two years (see p. 21). Relate these to your own work situation.

**5.** A review of workplace procedures is necessary because few women are prepared to make a formal complaint under the present system for fear of retaliation or of not being believed. The union is concerned to minimise the victim's distress and to deal with the issue in confidence in the first instance. This would also be in **management's interest** since the harasser may not be a co-worker but a supervisor or manager. The union's aim is to see the problem resolved, not to discipline workers automatically.

## Management policies

Persuading management to adopt a policy on sexual harassment at work is a crucial aspect of any campaign against sexism. Unless management accept sexual harassment as a legitimate issue for union/management action, unions will find themselves arguing about whether each and every complaint should be taken up as a genuine grievance. A management policy statement removes the issue from being one of a problem between individuals and clearly identifies sexual harassment as contrary to achieving equal opportunities and safe working conditions for women. Once the policy is agreed, unions can use the statement not only to take up individual grievances but to press management for a training programme aimed at eliminating sexist practices, including harassment, from the workplace.

How unions approach management to negotiate a workplace policy depends on whether or not an equal opportunities programme is already agreed. Most collective agreements make brief reference to non-discriminatory practices. For example, the **TUC model equal opportunities clause** states:

> The parties to this agreement are committed to the development of positive action programmes to promote equal opportunities in employment regardless of workers' sex, marital status, creed, colour, race or ethnic origin. This principle will apply in respect of all conditions of work including pay, hours of work, holiday entitlement, overtime and shift work, work allocation, guaranteed earnings, sick pay, pensions, recruitment, training, promotion and redundancy.
>
> The management undertake to draw opportunities for training and promotion to the attention of all eligible employees and to inform all employees of this agreement on equal opportunity.
>
> The parties agree that they will review from time to time, through their joint machinery, the operation of this equal opportunities policy.
>
> If any employee considers that he or she is suffering from unequal treatment on the grounds of sex, marital status, creed, colour, race or ethnic origins he or she may make a complaint which will be dealt with through the agreed procedures for dealing with grievances.

This or a similar clause is a useful first step in developing an equal opportunities policy, although some groups experiencing disadvantage at work are not covered by the TUC clause. You may therefore want to include a reference to people with disabilities, and gay and lesbian workers, by amending the first paragraph to read 'regardless of worker's sex, sexual orientation, marital status, creed, colour, race or ethnic origin, or physical disability'.

In taking up the issue of sexual harassment with management, an initial demand could be to **amend the equal opportunities clause** to include reference to sexual harassment as discriminatory behaviour. Such a statement, while limited, will enable the union to deal with complaints when they arise, as well as laying the basis for more detailed negotiation at a later stage. A form of words for such an amendment might be:

■ **Conduct by any employee, whether intentional or unintentional, that results in harassment of other employees on the grounds of their sex, race, or religion, is discriminatory and contrary to the company's commitment to equal opportunities and fair treatment for all its employees.**

While many unions have negotiated a general commitment from management for fair treatment for all workers, few agreements detail ways of achieving this, by for example introducing a positive action programme. In some workplaces, unions and management are discussing **specific measures for achieving equal opportunities** at work. Only changes in employment practices and the development of a positive action programme (as outlined in chapter 2) will improve the status and job opportunities of women workers. Negotiations should cover the provision of child-care, training, increasing opportunities for part-time work and job-sharing, better maternity rights and a review of recruitment and promotion procedures. To be effective, such a programme must also tackle the deeply-held sexist attitudes which undermine women's position at work. A commitment by management as well as the union to accept sexual harassment as discrimination against women and to combat sexist practices and attitudes within the workplace is an essential part of any detailed equal opportunities agreement.

Where unions have difficulty in persuading their employer to tackle sexual harassment as part of an equal opportunities programme, it may be possible to raise the issue on the grounds of health and safety at work. Under the Health and Safety at Work Act, employers are responsible for the health, safety and welfare of their employees. Sexual harassment causes a range of health problems, including migraine, tension, increased use of drugs, alcohol and cigarettes, sleeplessness and depression. Employers have a duty to eliminate health hazards from the workplace and to draw up a policy outlining how this will be done. Section 2(3) of the Health and Safety at Work Act states:

Except in such cases as may be prescribed, it shall be the duty of every employer to prepare and as often as may be appropriate revise, a written statement of his general policy with respect to the health and safety at work of his employees and the organisation and arrangements for the time being in force for carrying out that policy, and to bring the statement and any revisions of it to the notice of all his employees.

Unions could refer to 'a written statement of general policy' and 'the organisation and arrangements for the time being in force for carrying out that policy' to press management to introduce procedures covering sexual harassment.

Whether under the umbrella of health and safety or equal opportunities, a policy statement on sexual harassment should include:

- a definition of sexual harassment together with a clear indication of the types of behaviour which will be treated as such;
- reference to workplace procedures for dealing with complaints of sexual harassment;
- reference to the responsibility of managers and supervisors not only to treat complaints seriously but to actively combat sexist practices within the workplace;
- a commitment to provide a training programme for all employees to raise their awareness of sexism and sexual harassment, and including details of management policy on the issue.

In the USA, the government's industrial relations organisation has proposed a **model policy statement** for adoption by employers, which incorporates many of the points listed above.

### Excerpt from the National Labour Relations Board Policy, Administrative Policy Circular APC80–2, issued 21 February 1980

Sexual harassment is a form of employee misconduct which undermines the integrity of the employment relationship. All employees must be allowed to work in an environment free from unsolicited and unwelcome sexual overtures. Sexual harassment does not refer to the occasional compliment. It refers to behaviour which is not welcome, which is personally offensive, which debilitates morale and which therefore interferes with the work effectiveness of its victims and their co-workers. Sexual harassment may include actions such as:

- sex-orientated verbal 'kidding' or abuse;
- subtle pressure for sexual activity;
- physical contact such as patting, pinching, or constant brushing against another's body;
- demands for sexual favours, accompanied by implied or overt promises of preferential treatment or threats concerning an individual's employment status.

Sexual harassment is a prohibited personnel practice when it results in discrimination for or against an employee on the basis of conduct not related to work performance, such as the taking or refusal to take a personnel action including promotion of employees who submit to sexual advances or refusal to promote employees who resist or protest at sexual overtures.

Complaints of sexual harassment involving misuse of one's official position should be made orally or in writing to a higher level supervisor, to an appropriate personnel officer, or to anyone authorised to deal with discrimination complaints.

Because of the differences in employees' values and background, some individuals may find it difficult to recognise their own behaviour as sexual harassment. To create awareness of office conduct which may be construed as sexual harassment, we will incorporate sexual harassment training in future managerial, supervisory, equal opportunities, employee induction and other appropriate training courses. Additionally, a copy of this policy kit will be placed in each new employee induction kit.

In Britain, some unions are negotiating policies on sexual harassment but few yet appear to be concluded. The most comprehensive joint union/management statement to date comes from a civil service consultative committee, the Joint Review Group. It examined a range of issues associated with equal opportunities for women within the civil service, including sexual harassment. As other unions may find it useful to refer to the report's published recommendations during negotiations with their own employer, a lengthy extract is set out below.

### Equal Opportunities for Women in the Civil Service – a report by the Joint Review Group

#### *Sexual harassment*
7.6 In approaching this issue the group started from the premise that it is good personnel management practice to

ensure that there is a harmonious working environment in which all staff are treated equally as colleagues, irrespective of their sex. It was in this context that we considered the subject of sexual harassment at work. We were aware that although it is not a new problem it is an area where growing concern is being expressed, in the civil service as elsewhere. We believe that for all staff their working environment should be free of the unfair pressures of sexual harassment and that the civil service, like any responsible employer, will want to ensure this is so.

7.11 This brings us again to the problem of a definition of sexual harassment. We recognise that what one person regards as sexual harassment another may see as inoffensive. Nonetheless a working definition is essential and, in our view, it must clearly convey that sexual harassment constitutes actions which are deliberate, persistent, unreciprocated and unwelcome. These may include, but are not limited to, verbal threats or abuse, sexual mockery or innuendo, non-accidental touching, sexual assault, suggestions that sexual favours are a conditon of retention of jobs or of promotion, etc., and the display of sexually offensive or pornographic material in the workplace.

7.12 Staff at all levels need to be made aware that such actions are not acceptable. Managers, in particular, as well as setting a good example themselves should be ready to act promptly to deal with complaints of sexual harassment. In this respect, it is obviously important and necessary that those whose activities are complained of should receive a clear indication that their attentions are unwanted and unwelcome. The complainant may well feel intimidated in this and may need support from a friend, sympathetic colleague, union representative or welfare officer in drawing attention to the matter. All staff should be assured they can proceed, if necessary, with a formal complaint without fear of subsequent victimisation. The procedures for making a complaint should be clearly laid down and made known to all staff.

7.13 Finally, the group considered that a thorough survey should be undertaken into the nature and extent of sexual harassment in the civil service. In our view, it will not be sufficient to do this simply by the issue of questionnaires. We believe it is necessary for a sample of staff to be interviewed and that the sample should cover those employed in a whole range of civil service operational situations. It would seem appropriate for such a survey to take place under joint union/management supervision at National Whitley Council level with the enquiry work undertaken perhaps by an outside organisation (as was the case with the study of race relations in the civil service).

### Recommendations

7.14 We therefore recommend that:

(a) there should be a thorough survey to establish the nature and extent of harassment in the civil service;

(b) in the meantime;

(i) all civil servants should be made aware that sexual harassment at work will not be tolerated and, if appropriate, will be dealt with as a disciplinary matter;

(ii) a working definition of sexual harassment along the lines of paragraph 7.11 should be formulated and published to all staff;

(iii) managers should be made aware of their responsibilities both to set a good example and to deal promptly and fairly with complaints of sexual harassment;

(iv) staff should be made aware of the procedures for making formal complaints and should also be assured that they may proceed without fear of victimisation;

(v) staff should be clearly advised that in complaining of sexual harassment they must indicate their objection clearly to the offender and that in this they may have assistance from friends, colleagues, welfare officers or union representatives.

# Training programme

Once agreed, the policy statement should be **publicised throughout the workplace**. It is unlikely to be implemented, however, unless workers and management understand and support its contents. Adequate training must accompany the introduction of the policy and be continued at regular intervals afterwards. Sexual harassment at work cannot be dealt with in a single half-hour lecture; sexist behaviour will not cease simply by telling people it is unacceptable. Any training programme must offer an opportunity for workers and management to examine their own sexist attitudes and to recognise behaviour which discriminates against women. Unions should, therefore, negotiate over the **content of the training scheme** and may wish to take some responsibility for training their own members. Such training should stress the reasons for tackling sexual harassment, the procedures for taking up cases, and the approach of both management and union to the issue. Case studies and workplace problems, like those on pp. 91–5, could be adapted for this purpose.

A comprehensive management training programme should cover:

- definitions and examples of sexual harassment, and the consequences of harassment to both workers and employer;
- the necessity of tackling sexism and sexual harassment as part of providing equal opportunities at work for women;
- brief information on the legal background to harassment, the legal responsibilities of employers to remove discriminatory practices, and the uses and limitations of the law in tackling sexual harassment at work;
- management policy for combating sexism and sexual harassment, including the role of supervisors and managers in implementing the policy;
- formal and informal procedures for handling complaints, including the role of counselling and situations requiring disciplinary action;
- trade-union policies on sexual harassment and union involvement in workplace policies and procedures.

Those workers with responsibility for implementing management policies – foremen, supervisors and all grades of manager – should receive **detailed induction** into the requirements of the policy. Unions should ensure that training covers the range of problems likely to arise in implementing the policy. Once again, lectures are not enough; managers should be asked to tackle a variety of case studies of work situations related to sexism and sexual harassment. Unions who find their management reluctant to organise training can refer them to a number of recent articles in personnel management magazines, a list of which can be obtained from the Institute of Personnel Management. A few are included in the reading list at the end of the handbook. There are also an increasing number of courses about equal opportunities for women run by management training agencies. Some of these include activities aimed at tackling the negative and sexist attitudes of male managers towards women workers. A management training film, produced in the USA, is available from BNA Communications Europe (address at end of book) called *Preventing Sexual Harassment*. It examines management responsibilities and employee rights, and presents guidelines for dealing with incidents of sexual harassment. While referring to US laws, the case studies and the discussion of good management practices are relevant to this country.

## Procedures for handling complaints

Most unions have agreed procedures with management for handling workplace problems. These lay down rules for both union and management so that complaints and disciplinary offences are dealt with fairly and quickly. Complaints to management from members experiencing sexual harassment at work should fall within the terms of the grievance or disputes procedure. Anyone found to be harassing others at work may be dealt with under a disciplinary procedure. Unions need to **review these procedures** to ensure they are effective for tackling incidents of harassment. A number of points should be considered.

**1. Are members aware** that cases of sexual harassment can and will be dealt with through the normal grievance and disciplinary procedures? If not, should a statement to that effect be included in either or both agreements?

**2.** Should the grievance procedure include an **informal stage** for handling complaints of sexual harassment? Members may prefer to attend an informal, confidential discussion rather than a formal grievance hearing in the first instance. Union and management could seek a resolution of the problem at an early stage and avoid unnecessary disciplinary action. On the other hand, adopting an initial informal stage may lead management to assume the union is not interested in taking the issue seriously, or that the member's allegations are suspect since the union does not want them discussed formally.

**3.** Should the grievance procedure enable a woman filing a complaint of sexual harassment to be **represented by a woman** when her steward or convenor is a man? This could be a woman steward from another section of the workplace or a member of the union's equal opportunities committee. In either case, management would need to agree a change from normal practice.

**4.** Should the grievance procedure **refer complaints** of sexual harassment in the first instance **to a woman manager** designated by the employer to deal with cases, rather than taking them through normal procedures to the supervisor or line manager? Women may be reluctant to talk to a man about humiliating and embarrassing incidents, yet unless details are available, management may reject the allegations on the grounds of insufficient evidence. Where the woman's superior is the harasser, it would in any case be necesary to refer the complaint elsewhere.

**5.** Should members who harass others at work **be referred for counselling** as an alternative to being disciplined? Some members may be unaware that their behaviour causes distress. Management may have done little or nothing to educate their workforce about discriminatory behaviour. Under these circumstances, unions may prefer to give members time to improve before any warnings appear on their record.

Such an approach, while appearing fair, must not be seen as an easy option by either management or members. It must be made clear that *any* recurrence of the offence will be dealt with under the disciplinary procedure. Particularly serious cases of harassment should not, in any case, automatically go through an informal stage. Where unions decide to include counselling within their disciplinary procedure, they should negotiate a system with management. Unions may wish to nominate their own counsellor to work with management. Unions must ensure that management personnel responsible for counselling understand the nature and consequences of sexual harassment for women. Counsellors must be prepared both to explore and challenge the harasser's own attitudes to women and not simply demand that the offender 'keeps his nose clean'. Without safeguards, counselling could turn into a mechanism for protecting men from the serious consequences of their actions. As a result, women members will remain unconvinced that the union has any real commitment to tackling harassment and will prefer the harasser to be formally disciplined. On the other hand, successful counselling could have a far greater long-term impact on sexism at work than any number of verbal and written warnings.

Arising from these points, unions may or may not wish to amend their collective agreement to include reference to incidents of sexual harassment. Some unions have been reluctant to agree any specific offences as warranting disciplinary action so that they remain free to defend members irrespective of the charges against them. If this policy is continued, unions must reassure their women members that existing procedures can be used to tackle incidents of harassment, and that under no circumstances will the union condone discriminatory practices. Some unions, however, are negotiating new procedures for dealing with incidents of harassment and discrimination. Illustrated below are two sample agreements which other unions can adapt or amend to fit their own negotiating machinery. The first is a special grievance procedure to cover cases of sexual harassment.

■ **Grievance procedure for individuals and groups of employees for alleged sexual harassment**

*Introduction*
For the purposes of this procedure the definition of sexual harassment shall be used as follows:

> Any repeated and unwanted sexual comment, look, suggestion or physical contact that a person finds objectionable and offensive.

It can range from unwanted suggestions to attempted rape or rape. Physically it can include pinching, grabbing, hugging, patting, leering, brushing against and touching.

*Stage 1*
1. It is agreed that a trade-union member may seek advice from the union Equal Opportunities Officer or other representative at any time during the course of this procedure.
2. Wherever possible the employee(s) should ask the harasser to stop, or make it clear that the behaviour is unwelcome. However, this initial approach may be made by the trade-union representative.

*Stage 2*
1. If the complainant(s) is/are dissatisfied with the reply, or the harassment does not cease the employee(s) or trade-union representative shall take up the matter with the departmental personnel officer or, if inappropriate, with the designated officer within the central personnel department.
2. The personnel office shall reply orally as soon as possible (and in any case within two working days).
3. If the employee(s) continue(s) to be aggrieved, the individual or group or representative may submit the grievance to the personnel officer for transmission to the head of

department. The grievances may be put in writing on a form to be provided and available for that purpose. The employee(s) or representative shall keep at least one copy.

At this stage the personnel officer shall be responsible for notifying the person or persons accused that the matter is being taken further and that the accused has the right to seek trade-union representation.

### Stage 3

1. Where it is requested by one or both parties a pre-meeting may be called by the head of department with the representatives and personnel officer, to attempt to resolve the matter before proceeding.
2. The head of department (or senior representative) shall, within ten working days of receiving the complaint, call separate investigatory meetings with the complainant and the accused together with their representatives.
3. As soon as possible after this meeting the head of department shall give his judgement and notify any further action he will be taking, to both parties and their representatives writing.
4. If the head of department proposes any disciplinary action against either the complainant or the accused then the disciplinary procedure shall be entered.
5. If either party is dissatisfied with the judgement or non-disciplinary action taken by the head of department and/or continues to be aggrieved in respect of the original complaint, he or she shall have the right of appeal to the Appeals Panel.

### Final stage

1. The Appeals Panel shall be convened within ten working days after written request. The judgement of the Appeals Panel shall be communicated in writing to the appellant as soon as possible thereafter.

**Note:** Any reference to this procedure having been pursued to which has been entered on any employee(s) personal file shall be expunged after two years.

The key elements of this agreement are:

- members with complaints of sexual harassment can seek advice from the union's equal opportunities officer;
- if the victim so wishes, the union will approach the harasser with a request to stop;

- there is an opportunity for management to deal with the complaint informally before anything is put in writing;
- once a written complaint is made the alleged harasser has the right to be informed;
- before formal investigation takes place, an informal meeting can be held to try and resolve the problem;
- if appropriate, disciplinary action will be taken under the existing procedure;
- there is a right of appeal for both victim and harasser;
- any reference to the offence will be automatically removed from all files after two years.

The second sample agreement is part of an equal opportunities policy. The procedure is designed to cover all complaints of discrimination and unfair treatment, including sexual harassment; its purpose is to deal with **those cases of harassment and discrimination** (where inspired by the victim's sex or colour) **which may have no obvious detrimental consequences for the victim**. Under many grievance procedures a complaint of sexual harassment would not be accepted unless the victim had been harmed in some way. This procedure distinguishes between behaviour which results in specific acts of discrimination, such as lack of promotion, and practices which distress and humiliate the victim, for example a sexual comment or pornographic graffiti, but which involve no clearly identifiable loss of job opportunity.

■ **Procedure for dealing with complaints of discrimination and unfair treatment**

### *Nature of the complaint*
An employee's complaint would fall into one of two categories:

- an allegation of racial or sexual discrimination or harassment;
- a grievance for which redress is sought that there has been unfair treatment on the grounds of sex or race which has led to some form of loss (e.g. pay, promotion, etc.).

Where cases are brought under both headings it will be treated first as an allegation. If necessary the complainant can pursue the grievance after the allegation has been investigated. It is likely that should the allegation be proved, the grievance would be redressed.

### Procedure for dealing with allegations

1. The employee alleging racial or sexual discrimination or harassment should make a formal complaint in writing to their head of department.
2. On receiving the complaint, the head of department will hold an enquiry, to include a discussion with the complainant who may be accompanied by a trade-union representative.
3. When the enquiry is complete, the head of department should inform the person bringing the complaint of the result. If a disciplinary offence has been committed, proceedings should be taken against the offender under the disciplinary procedure.

### Procedure for dealing with grievances

A grievance for which a redress is sought will be dealt with under the normal grievance procedure.

### Amendment to disciplinary procedure

1. Discriminatory acts are, for disciplinary purposes defined as actions which have the effect of treating employees less favourably on the grounds of sex, race, colour, nationality, ethnic or national origins, marital status, sexual orientation, age, trade-union activity, political or religious belief.
2. Sexual harassment, for disciplinary purposes, is defined as repeated, unwanted, unreciprocated and unwelcome comments, looks, actions, suggestions, or physical contact that is objectionable and offensive to the recipient and that might threaten the employee's job security or create an intimidating working environment.

In this agreement:

- union and management are making a firm commitment to tackle all forms of sexist and racist abuse in the workplace;
- a complaint of sexual harassment could be investigated in two stages:
  - (i) as an allegation, to determine whether or not sexual harassment of any kind has occurred;
  - (ii) if the allegation was proved, the complaint would also be treated as a grievance if the victim had suffered an obvious loss of opportunity;
- the list of existing disciplinary offences has been amended to cover acts of discrimination and sexual harassment.

A workplace agreement for handling cases of sexual harassment not only provides members with a procedure which is of practical benefit but the negotiations offer a legitimate method of bringing the issue to management attention. Managements are well aware of union reluctance to amend a well-tried procedure unnecessarily; unions who approach their employer for an agreement will be showing how seriously the union regards harassment as a problem for its members. But signing a joint agreement is only one step in any campaign to combat sexist practices at work. Unions have a responsibility to ensure that agreed policies and procedures are adhered to by both management and members. The efforts involved in negotiating the agreement will be wasted without continued activity by the union to identify and overcome all forms of sexism in the workplace.

# 7.

# Using the law

Relevant law / sex discrimination / unfair dismissal / health and safety at work / criminal and civil courts / claiming sex discrimination / claiming unfair dismissal / legal advice.

Women who are sexually harassed at work and who are unable to tackle the problem within their workplace may find a remedy by taking legal action against their harasser. Important as this option is, **it offers a solution in only a minority of cases**. The law is a blunt instrument since it can only deal with cases which clearly fall within the terms of reference of the relevant act. For some types of sexual harassment, such as whistling or displaying soft porn, the law offers no remedy. Taking legal action is not in any case an easy decision for a woman. Not unnaturally, many are reluctant to have distressing aspects of their working life put on public show, particularly given the media appetite for salacious comment on any story connected with sex. It may be difficult to assemble satisfactory evidence or persuade friends and colleagues to act as witnesses. Women may face discrimination at the hearing, where the majority of participants are likely to be men with little understanding or sympathy for victims of sexual harassment.

Despite these limitations, the law can offer a remedy in extreme situations where no other form of action is available. It is particularly important for those women in workplaces which lack trade-union organisation or satisfactory procedures for dealing with complaints. Although not everyone who experiences harassment in these circumstances will finally take legal action, a victim's knowledge of the law may help discourage the harasser. Few men realise the extent to which their sexist behaviour could involve them in expensive litigation. This chapter sets out:

- **the various laws related to sexual harassment;**
- **how these laws can be used;**

- **examples of cases which have been heard;**
- **how to make a claim;**
- **where to get legal advice on sexual harassment.**

At the time of writing, there have only been a few legal actions involving sexual harassment in Britain. Over the last year there has been considerable debate within the legal profession about the most satisfactory way of taking up the issue. Much of this has centred on the extent to which the experiences in the USA might be relevant to British law. The information in this chapter draws on the best opinions to date, but **it is difficult to give conclusive advice on the likely outcome** of any subsequent legal action on the issue. For this reason alone, anyone contemplating taking legal action should seek advice from one of the agencies listed at the end of this chapter.

## Relevant law

Sexual harassment at work involves an action taken by an individual or group of individuals against others in the workplace. How the law is used depends on the consequences of harassment, and in some cases more than one remedy may be appropriate. To date, the majority of cases have been heard under the law relating to unfair dismissal laid down in the Employment Protection (Consolidation) Act 1978. This involves the person dismissed bringing a claim against her employer to the industrial tribunal. In cases of sexual harassment, a woman may also be able to bring a claim against her employer under the Sex Discrimination Act 1975 (SDA); **while no such complaints have yet been heard by a tribunal**, a number have been filed and may be dealt with at a later date. In the future, the use of the SDA seems the more likely remedy for sexual harassment since that law can take account of employers' actions short of dismissal which result in discrimination against women. In the USA, actions under their equivalent act have resulted in large financial settlements for women subjected to harassment.

Although harassment takes place at work, there is no reason why either the criminal or civil law should not be used if the behaviour amounts to assault, rape or an attempt at either. However, the criminal law has proved unsatisfactory for dealing with many cases where women are sexually assaulted, particularly where there are no witnesses, and harassment at work is likely to be no exception. Finally, it can be argued that stress caused by harassment arises from an unsatisfactory and unsafe working environment, a situation which comes within the terms of the Health and Safety at Work Act 1974. While workers may be able to use this act during workplace negotiations on the issue of harassment, it is uncertain how far the Health and Safety Executive would agree to enforce the act to cover sexual harassment at work.

## Sexual harassment as sex discrimination

The Sex Discrimination Act outlaws discrimination on the grounds of sex and marital status in employment, housing, education and services. It applies equally to women and men. Despite being law since 1975, no cases of discrimination due to sexual harassment have yet been heard under the act. However, the Equal Opportunities Commission, together with a number of lawyers and other legal agencies, consider that the act can be used for this purpose since its clauses are similar to those of Title VII of the US Civil Rights Act 1964, which has proved a useful support for victims of harassment. A number of cases have been filed under the SDA but settled out of court, often because neither employer nor victim wanted embarrassing information discussed publicly. Initiating a case under the SDA, without taking it to the final tribunal stage, can act as a warning to the employer to stop the discriminatory action. How to do this is outlined later in this chapter. The first case likely to be heard by a tribunal will be used as a test case, so the evidence needs to be so strong that the case cannot fail. It would set an unfortunate precedent if a tribunal ruled that sexual harassment was not discrimination on the grounds of sex, and this was then upheld on appeal to the Employment Appeal Tribunal.

Since it seems likely in the future that the SDA will offer women the most useful legal mechanism for seeking redress against sexual harassment, this section examines in some detail how the law would need to be used. Achieving a tribunal ruling under the SDA in favour of the victim of sexual harassment depends on the legal interpretation of those parts of the act relevant to discrimination in employment. It will be necessary to show:

- that sexual harassment is discrimination on the grounds of sex;
- that sexual harassment is unlawful behaviour;

- that an employer is liable for harassment taking place in his/her workplace.

Establishing these same points was important in the USA, where a number of cases helped to create a legal approach to harassment sympathetic to the victim. While US rulings cannot be used directly when presenting evidence to an industrial tribunal in Britain, anyone at present thinking of filing a complaint of discrimination on the grounds of sexual harassment under the SDA must be prepared to argue about the same legal principles.

## Sex discrimination

To establish that sexual harassment is discrimination on the grounds of sex depends on clarifying various aspects of the law. The first is that sexual harassment occurs **because the victim is a woman and is for this reason treated less favourably** than a man. Section 1(1) of the SDA states:

> Any person discriminates against a woman in any circumstances relevant for the purposes of any provision of this Act if – (a) on the grounds of her sex he treats her less favourably than he treats or would treat a man.

The second aspect to be established is that discrimination can arise when **some women**, rather than all women, **are in fact so treated**. Thirdly, it must be shown that men and women **are employed in similar circumstances** such that a comparison of their situations can be made.

In the USA, some of the early cases were lost because the courts ruled that a particular woman was harassed **not because she was a woman** but because as an individual **she was personally attractive** to the harasser. In *Corne and DeVane v Bausche and Lomb* (390 F.Supp. 191 D.Ariz. 1975) the claim of discrimination failed because the judge held that the harassment was the result of a **personal urge** on the part of the supervisor towards two women, and not undertaken because of the employers' policy. He went on to express concern about the implications of accepting such cases as discrimination, fearing there would be a lawsuit every time an employee made amorous or sexually-orientated advances towards another', and he added, 'the only way an employer could avoid such charges was to have employees who were asexual'.

Designating harassment as a personal problem rather than a

workplace issue affecting women was tested in a US court of appeal in the case of *Barnes v Costle* (13 FEP Cases 123 DDC 1974). Paulette Barnes, a wages clerk, had complained that her supervisor tried to extract sexual favours from her, including demands for dates and a suggestion that she would be promoted if she co-operated in an affair. Following her firm refusal, the supervisor belittled and harassed her, demoted her and finally abolished her job. Her first claim of sex discrimination was unsuccessful; the court ruled that she was penalised not because of her sex but because she refused her supervisor's advances. However, the court of appeal recognised that her supervisor only demanded sexual favours **because she was a woman** and he would not have treated a man in the same way. The judgement stated:

> but for her womanhood, her participation in sexual activity would never have been solicited. To say then that she was victimised in her employment simply because she declined the invitation is to ignore the asserted fact that **she was invited only because she was a woman** subordinate to the inviter in the hierarchy of agency personnel. Put another way, she became the target of the supervisor's sexual desires because she was a woman and was asked to bow to his demands as the price for holding her job.

Such arguments should be used to establish under section 1(1)(a) of the SDA that a woman is subjected to harassment because of her sex. It will be necessary also to argue that sex discrimination arises when only some women are discriminated against, since it is unlikely that all women in a workplace will have been harassed. The only case in Britain in which this was a central question was that of *Hurley v Mustoe* (1981 IRLR), where Ms Hurley, a waitress, was sacked not because she was a woman, but because she was a woman with small children. The employer did employ women without children. The Employment Appeal Tribunal supported the claim of sex discrimination on the basis that it was a condition applied to women but not to men, even though not all women were affected. It seems likely, therefore, that other cases of sex discrimination not involving all the women at a workplace would be treated in the same way.

There is one further hurdle in establishing whether sexual harassment cases can be dealt with under the SDA. Section 5(3) of the act demands that in comparing the treatment of women and men, **their circumstances must be the same or not materially**

**different**. For example, in a case of sexual harassment resulting in lack of promotion for a woman it would be necessary to show that her qualifications and experience were identical, or better than those of a man. An employer might, however, try to argue that their circumstances were not similar because men lack the qualities which inspire sexual interest! In the case of *Turley v Alders Dept Store* (1980 IRLR), it was held that dismissing Ms Turley because she was pregnant was not discrimination on the grounds of sex because men cannot get pregnant. Similarly, it might be argued that male and female sexuality are different and cannot be compared. Counter to this is the view that under the SDA an employer cannot make relevant to the comparison characteristics of workers, such as their sexual attractiveness, which have nothing to do with job performance.

These legal arguments indicate that the SDA could be used in cases of sexual harassment. Until legal precedents are set, any woman or her legal adviser claiming unfavourable treatment due to harassment needs to take note of these points in preparing a case for the tribunal:

- sexual harassment is part of the working environment of women because they are women, and similar treatment is not directed at men – there is, therefore, a prima facie case of sex discrimination;
- sex discrimination does arise where only some women, but not all, because of their sex, are subjected to unfavourable treatment, i.e. the effects of harassment;
- since sexuality is not a criterion for job performance, a sex discrimination claim should not be rejected on the grounds that male and female sexuality constitute a material difference between women and men.

**'Less favourable treatment'**

The SDA demands a proof not only that a woman is treated differently from a man but also that this treatment is less favourable. Less favourable treatment in employment is defined in section 6 of the act and covers offers of employment, terms and conditions of employment, access to opportunities and benefits at work, dismissal and 'any other detriment'. To prove discrimination on the grounds of sexual harassment it would be necessary to show that the consequences to the women arising from harassment come within at least one of these categories.

The most obvious cases are those where a refusal to comply with sexual demands has led to retaliation, such as lack of promotion, dismissal, or reduction in pay. It may be more difficult to prove a 'detriment' where sexual harassment is part of the working environment but no tangible employment benefits are lost. However, some lawyers believe that a workplace in which women are subject to hostile and intimidating behaviour, such as touching, leering, sexual remarks, could be classed as a detriment. In the USA such a broad definition was accepted in the case of *Bundy v Jackson* (24 FEP Cases 1155, 1981), where the court ruled that sexually stereotyped remarks and propositions directed at Ms Bundy, and which caused her anxiety, did constitute sex discrimination even though she suffered no economic disadvantage. Thus where harassment results in poor work performance, stress, sickness or unwillingness to undertake certain jobs, 'detriment' may be clearly established. The tribunal is, however, likely to regard as frivolous cases of harassment in which a woman objects to sexist attitudes and behaviour at her workplace, but has not suffered in any material sense.

In preparing a case for the tribunal it will be important to establish clearly the type of 'detriment' suffered by the victim of harassment. Evidence such as a medical certificate, work records before and after harassment commenced, witnesses' accounts of the effect of harassment on the victim both at work and outside will help to clarify the nature of the 'detriment'. In countering allegations of harassment, an employer is likely to argue that any actions taken against the victim arose from work-related factors such as absenteeism, a bad sickness record or inability to do the job competently. Refuting such charges will be easier if documentary and eye-witness accounts can be produced, although in at least one case of unfair dismissal related to sexual harassment the tribunal accepted the woman's unsupported evidence. At the same time a victim must be prepared to counter arguments about their own psychological instability and over-sensitivity to a casual remark or friendly gesture. Members of tribunals, most of whom are men, are as imbued with sexist attitudes and behaviour as any group of workers; in pleading that unfavourable treatment has occurred as the result of sexual harassment, they will need convincing that harassment is a serious issue for women.

The following **checklist** identifies situations which could be used to establish 'detriment' arising from sexual harassment:

Action by the employer (or employer's agent):
- refused employment;
- dismissal;
- lack of promotion;
- refused training;
- refused regrading, or down-graded;
- refused overtime or bonus opportunities;
- moved to less satisfactory work;
- worsening of working conditions;
- poor job performance rating;
- refused 'perks' available to others;
- refused references or given poor reference.

Effects on the victim:
- absenteeism;
- sickness;
- stress;
- feelings of humiliation and reduction in confidence;
- unwillingness to work with harasser;
- request for transfer;
- forced to leave.

## Employer's liability

Under the SDA, any claim of less favourable treatment on the grounds of sex discrimination is made against the employer. Section 41(1) states that 'anything done by a person in the course of his employment shall be treated . . . as done by his employer as well as by him, *whether or not* it was done with the employer's knowledge and approval'. In cases of sex discrimination by a co-worker or supervisor, the employer is therefore held legally liable.

Cases in the USA involving sexual harassment have attempted to define this liability. In *Miller v Bank of America* (600 F. 2d 211, 1979) the bank stated that there was a company policy condemning this type of conduct. The judge ruled that the existence of the policy reduced the employer's liability since the victim had not used it to request an investigation into the alleged harassment. The policy required 'all known and pertinent facts concerning possible improper actions or behaviour should be reported immediately'; thus although there was no specific mention of sexual harassment constituting an improper act, the employer was able to use the existence of a general procedure to show an intention to remove discriminatory practices.

Other US cases have established that to limit liability an employer must state specifically that sexual harassment is unlawful, set up procedures for dealing with complaints and specify disciplinary measures to be used against a harasser. To assist employers, the US Equal Employment Opportunities Commission has produced guidelines on sexual harassment under Title VII of the Civil Rights Act. These provide a code of practice for dealing with harassment and lay down the degree of employer liability:

> With respect to conduct between fellow employees, an employer is responsible for acts of sexual harassment in the workplace where the employer (or its agents or supervisory employees) knows or should have known of the conduct unless it can show that it took immediate and appropriate corrective action.

Section 41(3) of the SDA states that the liability of employers in Britain for discriminatory acts by their employees depends on whether they have taken all 'reasonably practicable' steps to prevent discrimination. Going by the US experience, employers policies, however ineffective, could constitute 'reasonable steps'. Before taking a case to the tribunal, it will be necessary to establish **what policies and procedures exist in the workplace** for dealing with harassment. A tribunal might consider a normal grievance or complaints procedure adequate even though it makes no specific mention of sexual harassment. In this situation, arguments as to why the procedure was not used, or evidence to show that complaints were not dealt with seriously will help counter a defence of non-liability from the employer.

To sum up, taking action under the SDA could offer a remedy to women who experience harassment. Where sexual harassment is clearly associated with less favourable treatment, there is some chance of success. In such cases, victims of harassment will receive compensation from their employer, who will be required to ensure similar instances do not occur again. Already, a few employers have been prepared to settle a case in advance of the tribunal hearing rather than have the case discussed in public. Legal action is not, however, a suitable mechanism for dealing with subtler forms of harassment where sexist attitudes and behaviour undermine the position of women as workers but which cannot easily be linked to specific instances of discrimination.

# Sexual harassment and unfair dismissal

Industrial tribunals *have* dealt with cases of sexual harassment arising from unfair dismissal applications under the Employment Protection (Consolidation) Act 1978. On the surface this appears a more straightforward procedure than claiming sex discrimination since the law in this field is well-established. However, claiming unfair dismissal is only relevant to those cases of harassment which result in an employer **sacking** the victim or where the woman finds she has **no option but to leave**. While dismissal arising from harassment can produce claims for both unfair dismissal and sex discrimination, all other forms of unfavourable treatment must be dealt with under the SDA. In the majority of unfair dismissal cases, the tribunal **has not ruled on the alleged harassment**, but only on the fairness or otherwise of the dismissal.

## What is unfair dismissal?

Dismissal occurs when an employer **sacks a woman with or without notice**. This may be the result of her refusal to comply with harassment, because she has created problems in the workplace by complaining about harassment, or because she has taken time off work as a result of harassment. Section 57 of the 1978 act lays down the circumstances in which such a sacking would be legal. The act specifies that a dismissal would be potentially fair if the employer can show substantial reason for the dismissal related to the dismissed person's **capability, qualifications or conduct**. This has been amended so that:

> the determination of the question whether the dismissal is fair or unfair, having regards to the reason shown by the employer, shall depend on whether in the circumstances (including the **size and administrative resources** of the employer's undertaking), the employer acted reasonably or unreasonably in treating it as **sufficient reason** for dismissing the employee.

It is up to the tribunal to decide, therefore, not only whether the employer had a justified reason, but also whether it was an adequate reason for sacking someone given the type of workplace. Since many women work in small workplaces, the proviso to take the employer's size and administrative resources into account makes women particularly likely to lose claims for unfair dismissal.

A woman who is forced to leave her job because of sexual

harassment is entitled to claim **constructive dismissal**. Legally this refers to a situation where the employer shows by his words or actions that he no longer intends to be bound by one or more of the essential terms of the contract of employment. While the most obvious cases occur where a worker suffers a cut in pay or a reduction in status, it can be argued that a harassment-free workplace is an implicit term within the employment contract. This is certainly the view of Lord Justice Lawton, summing up an Appeal Court hearing in the case of *Western Excavation (ECC) Ltd v Sharp* (1978 IRLR) (a constructive dismissal case not related to sexual harassment). He stated:

> Sensible persons have no difficulty in recognising conduct by an employer which under law brings a contract of employment to an end. Persistent and unwanted amorous advances by an employer to a female member of staff would, for example, **clearly be such conduct**.

## Cases of unfair dismissal

There have been a number of cases of unfair dismissal involving allegations of sexual harassment in which the tribunal ruled in favour of the victim. However, as the examples show, the tribunal in each case avoided passing judgement on whether or not sexual harassment at work is an unacceptable practice, and concentrated on the procedures used for effecting the dismissal.

■ **Example:** Vicky Stevans, a clerk-typist with Powerflame Combustion Services Ltd, was dismissed without notice on the morning of 25 February 1980 by Mr Game, a company managing director. Ms Stevans had complained to another member of the office staff, a Ms Welsh, that Mr Game had acted improperly towards her. At the tribunal, Ms Stevans said that a number of incidents took place from August 1979 onwards. On one occasion Mr Game had asked whether she was wearing a bra. On another he had come up behind her, lifted her up and touched her breasts. Subsequently he had fiddled with her skirt zip and attempted to kiss her. She had reported these incidents to Ms Welsh. (IT 5435/80)

In considering Ms Stevans' claim for unfair dismissal, the tribunal argued that **allegations of sexual harassment could be reasonable grounds for dismissal**, depending on the size of the workplace. They stated:

Once the allegations are made in a smaller office and a small concern of this kind a situation is arrived at which is described, and we would agree, as intolerable and that this therefore meant **there would have to be a parting of the ways**. This could be done by Miss Stevans herself resigning or of course it could be done by her dismissal after due enquiry and after all the circumstances had been sifted. Therefore, there could be a reasonable ground for dismissal in this case.

Despite this statement, the tribunal supported Ms Stevans' claim for unfair dismissal. They ruled that as the allegations of sexual harassment were a highly personal matter between her and Mr Game, he should not have been the person to dismiss her. The claim was upheld because the **dismissal had not been arrived at in a reasonable way**, although the reason for the dismissal was considered fair. A similar argument was used by the tribunal in another case.

- **Example:** Sally Handley, employed as a steward at Teddington Conservative Club, was dismissed on 1 September 1980 due to absence through sickness. She had been sick for one month, suffering from nervous tension brought on by the persistent offensive and unmannerly behaviour of a group of club members, including committee members. On the evening prior to falling sick she had tried to calm down one member of the club who was behaving abusively to the club stewardess. She received her notice several hours after her doctor signed her fit for work. (IT 28933/80/B)

The tribunal agreed with the employer that it was difficult for the club to operate without a steward. However, they ruled that the club management committee should have found out how long Ms Handley was likely to be sick before giving her notice, and on these grounds they upheld her claim. At no time did the tribunal comment on the reasons for Ms Handley's absence, or suggest that an employer has a responsibility to provide a harassment-free workplace. The sacking was unfair because of **the way it was done**, not because prolonged sickness due to stress at work was considered an unjustified reason for dismissal.

There has also been a case of constructive dismissal involving sexual harassment.

- **Example:** Julie Hyatt, a clerk employed by Smithko of Salop Ltd, claimed constructive dismissal on the ground of the offensive behaviour of Mr Smith, a managing director with the company. She said that he pinched her bottom, put his arms round her, tried to kiss her, asked what her favourite position was, and what she wore in bed. Matters came to a head on 20 October 1980 when she objected to a remark about her nipple. Mr Smith stated she was lucky to work in such a friendly environment. She resigned immediately. (IT 00104/81)

In this instance, the tribunal was reluctant to support the claim for constructive dismissal. The chairman said he was unimpressed with Ms Hyatt's evidence, for which she had no witnesses except her husband, who had seen her come home very distressed on a number of occasions. However, the chairman agreed to uphold her claim because the assessors, who look at the case before the formal hearing, had considered the evidence adequate.

The way these tribunals handled cases suggests that as yet the law is unwilling to recognise sexual harassment at work as a legitimate grievance. Harassment was treated as a personal problem between two people and not a workplace issue; the right of the employer to dismiss in this situation was not challenged, particularly where the workplace was small. The only requirement was for managements to use proper dismissal procedures. Such rulings give support to employers who use dismissal as an easy way of solving workplace problems, so long as they do so via a formal procedure.

On the evidence of these cases, women claiming unfair dismissal associated with sexual harassment would be advised to base their claim wherever possible as much on the way the dismissal was handled as on the facts of the harassment. In a constructive dismissal claim, however, the evidence of sexual harassment will be **central** to the case. The claimant will have to show that the employer's behaviour, or that of his employee, was such as to constitute a breach of the contract of employment. It would therefore be unwise for a woman to resign after only one incident; the tribunal is more likely to support the claim if harassment has continued for some considerable time, providing a **protest has been made to the employer**. If no protest is made, the tribunal would query why the woman appeared prepared to work for some period without taking any action. On resigning, the employer should be informed in writing of the reasons for doing so and that these are grounds for a constructive dismissal claim.

# Health and safety at work

Sexual harassment is a major health hazard for women at work, because of the **stress** generated in coping with harassment – whether from making a complaint or trying to put up with it. As well as immediate symptoms such as headaches and nausea, stress causes long-term damage to a person's physical health by increasing both the likelihood of stomach, heart and nervous diseases, and dependency on drugs, alcohol or cigarettes. Stress can also lead to difficulties in maintaining family and social relationships, and increases the chances of mental breakdown. Not unnaturally perhaps, women who are subject to sexual harassment outside the home may be afraid to go out to meet new people.

Stress has consequences not only for the sufferer but also for other people they live and work with. At work a person under stress is likely to work more slowly or erratically, and make more mistakes. Tiredness and an inability to concentrate cause accidents at work. As a result, it is in the interests of all workers to ensure that their workplace is free from activities which cause stress, including sexual harassment.

In law, health and safety at work is primarily the **responsibility of the employer**, although employees must take reasonable care to ensure they do not endanger themselves or anyone else who may be affected by their work activities. Under section 2(2)(e) of the Health and Safety at Work Act 1974, the employer must undertake:

> the provision and maintenance of a working environment for his employees that is, so far as is reasonably practicable, safe, **without risk to health**, and adequate as regards facilities and arrangements for their welfare at work.

In carrying out this responsibility, an employer should take steps to ensure a stress-free working environment by tackling a range of stress-generating factors, to include not only the organisation and speed of work, but also those actions of his employees which distress and humiliate other workers.

While there is therefore a general legal requirement on the employer to promote a healthy workplace, there are in practice **considerable problems in legally enforcing these provisions**. The Health and Safety Executive (HSE) is empowered to order employers, through enforcement notices or legal action, to comply with those parts of health and safety law which lay down specific minimum standards. While the HSE would also consider it necessary for employers to adhere to the broader requirements of the act, they have to date taken a few steps to demand compliance unless workers have already sustained injury or other obvious ill health. The HSE has not taken up sexual harassment at work as a health and safety hazard; how far they would be willing in individual cases to persuade employers to treat sexual harassment as coming under the terms of the Health and Safety at Work Act may well depend on the views of the individual HSE inspectors. Occupational health is also the responsibility of the Employment Medical Advisory Service (EMAS) which researches into work-related illnesses. Despite the accumulation of evidence linking work-generated stress to various diseases, EMAS has undertaken very little research into occupational stress. At present therefore they, like the HSE, appear unlikely to support workers who approach them about cases of sexual harassment at work.

While the provisions of the Health and Safety at Work Act may not, as yet, be legally enforceable for cases of sexual harassment, the act may provide a useful argument **within the workplace** for workers to press their employer to take action against sexual harassment. The health and safety aspects of harassment may encourage the employer to take the issue seriously, particularly if he is made aware of the possible costs involved, through sickness and poor work performance resulting from harassment. Under the act, employers are expected to provide a health and safety policy; guidelines for dealing with sexual harassment could come under this umbrella (see chapter 6). At national level a number of trade unions are dealing with sexual harassment as part of their health and safety policies on the grounds that employers are more easily persuaded to negotiate health and safety matters than to introduce equal opportunities measures or amend disputes and disciplinary procedures.

## Using the criminal and civil courts

While the most usual remedies for sexual harassment at work are likely to come from using employment law, serious incidents of harassment might also involve criminal or civil law procedures. The sex discrimination act and the unfair dismissal provisions are aimed at redressing a **tangible wrong done to the victim** by her employer, and may not therefore be a suitable mechanism for pursuing incidents of sexual harassment which have no obvious work-related detrimental consequences for the victim. Criminal and civil law, on the other hand, is based on whether the **nature of the offender's behaviour** to the victim is a wrongful act, thereby emphasising what the harasser has done rather than exactly how the victim has been affected. These procedures may, therefore, offer a more effective means of dealing with harassment where, for example, a co-worker is pestering a woman outside the workplace, or where action is needed more quickly than can be achieved by applying to an industrial tribunal.

A serious case of sexual harassment could involve the criminal or civil courts by:

- the police prosecuting the harasser in the Magistrates or Crown Court for committing a criminal offence, for which, if guilty, he would be punished;
- the victim suing the harasser in the County Court for damages arising out of an assault or intent to cause harm, with the option also of obtaining an injunction restraining the harasser from repeating his behaviour towards the victim.

Criminal offences related to sexual harassment could involve complete or attempted acts of **assault, battery, actual and grievous bodily harm, indecent assault and rape**. Assault and battery could cover incidents of harassment such as being forcibly pushed into a cupboard and fondled; being attacked and injured by a co-worker on the way home could result in a charge of actual or grievous bodily harm. For sexual harassment to constitute indecent assault, the harasser **must do more** than make an indecent invitation or suggestion, by, for example, actually touching or making as if to touch the victim in circumstances which are considered indecent. Rape covers only those incidents of sexual assault where a man forcibly penetrates a woman's vagina with his penis.

Although men who seriously harass women should be prosecuted, many women are reluctant to make a complaint of sexual assault to the police, either for fear that it will not be treated seriously, or because they know their attacker well. Any woman who has been violently assaulted at work and who is unsure about contacting the police can approach their nearest Rape Crisis Centre for support (see p. 66). The police often appear reluctant to press charges where the person committing the offence is known to the victim. This is particularly true where a woman is battered by the man she lives with, since the offence is treated as a personal problem between two people. It is not clear how far the police would take a similar view in deciding whether or not to prosecute in a serious case of sexual assault occurring within a workplace. While there is no legal reason why they should not bring charges, doing so may well depend on the availability of witnesses able and willing to corroborate the victim's account.

Where the police decide not to prosecute an offender, the victim can take out a private prosecution for assault. A private prosecution is, however, very risky. The person bringing the case is not entitled to legal aid and, depending on the outcome of the trial, could be made to pay all or some of the legal costs. Despite this drawback victims have occasionally brought their own case against an offender. Two women recently won cases they were forced to bring themselves: one in Scotland was the victim of a multiple rape; the other was badly beaten by a gang of white youths in the east end of London. The police had decided not to prosecute in either case, even though in both instances the offences were committed by strangers. Although these women were successful, victims of serious harassment who find the police reluctant to pursue their case would probably find it safer to claim in the civil court for damages against the harasser rather than consider a private prosecution.

In cases of sexual harassment where the offender pleads not guilty and is brought to trial in the Crown Court for indecent assault, the victim of sexual harassment will need to satisfy the jury beyond reasonable doubt that **she did not consent** to the behaviour and that the act of the offender was **hostile**. Touching someone's body in passing is unlikely to meet these conditions; a case might succeed where a woman was forcibly detained and her breasts fondled. The usual defence used by men charged with rape or indecent assault is that they believed the victim consented to their sexual demands. Commonly held attitudes that 'certain women ask for it' and 'women like to play hard to get' often result in the victim, rather than the accused, finding her behaviour and character on trial. In cases of sexual harassment, it may be relatively easy for the harasser to suggest consent, since he may have known the victim for a long time and the incident for which he is being prosecuted may only be the most serious of many. As with claims under employment law, evidence that a woman **previously complained** about harassment could be vital in establishing her lack of consent. Given these difficulties, few women may be willing to face the glare of publicity involved in a court hearing, or the humiliation of being cross-examined about their sexual behaviour.

An alternative to a police prosecution is for the victim of sexual harassment to **sue the harasser** in the County Court for damages arising from an assault. Legal aid is available to do this. Civil procedures are used frequently in disputes between neighbours, where, as with sexual harassment, both victim and harasser may know each other well. A common assault does not automatically require violent physical contact, but only **the intention to use force or to cause physical harm**. Under this latter provision, damages have been awarded to individuals who suffered severe nervous shock as a result of a practical joke. A victim of sexual harassment who experiences stress and sickness as a result of the harasser's behaviour may well be able to make a similar claim, although there is very little information about the actual use of the civil law for cases of sexual harassment at work.

A victim of assault may find some advantage in bringing a civil case as compared to having the matter dealt with in the criminal court. In a criminal prosecution the evidence must show 'beyond reasonable doubt' that the accused committed the offence; in determining whether or not a claim for damages is justified, the court must decide **'on the balance of probability'** that the alleged assault took place. It may be easier for a victim of sexual harassment to show that she was **unlikely** to have consented to the harasser's advances, which therefore constitute a common assault, than to prove **absolutely** that she did not.

When seeking damages for assault, the victim of harassment could also apply for an **injunction** ordering the harasser not to repeat his behaviour. Injunctions are granted to women who are beaten by the men they live with; breaking an injunction is contempt of court for which the offender can be punished by imprisonment. The terms of the injunction would depend on the circumstances of the case. A woman followed home regularly and pestered by a co-worker might request an injunction to require the harasser to come no closer to her than 50 feet; where the harassment occurred at work, the order might state that the offender is not to touch the victim. As with other legal measures, using this provision will depend on the circumstances in which the harassment took place. Because the law has, as yet, rarely been used to deal with cases of sexual harassment, a woman considering bringing a civil action should seek legal advice.

A woman who has suffered serious physical injury, such as a damaged vagina or an arm broken in a struggle to get away as the result of a violent physical assault, may be eligible to claim **compensation** from the Criminal Injuries Compensation Board (CICB, address at end of book). This is a state-run body which pays compensation to people injured as a result of crime. Payment does not depend on anyone being prosecuted or convicted of the offence, but the CICB will not pay unless the crime was immediately reported to the police. To make a claim, a woman injured by someone she knows must be willing to identify her attacker. Where the harasser was a client or customer this may prove easier to do than when the crime has been committed by a co-worker the victim knows well, and who may have the support of other members of the workforce. Application forms are available from the CICB.

Women experiencing sexual harassment at work are likely to find the criminal and civil courts appropriate for dealing with only a very small minority of incidents of harassment at work. Where an incident involves serious assault, criminal or civil action could proceed alongside a claim of sex discrimination or unfair dismissal, so that a victim might be able to obtain compensation from her employer as well as damages from the harasser. However, until more cases come before the courts, it is difficult to determine under exactly what circumstances the different legal remedies can be most effectively used.

## Making a claim under the Sex Discrimination Act

Many people are put off by the complex machinery of law from obtaining redress for legitimate grievances. This section explains the practical issues involved in making a complaint of sex discrimination associated with sexual harassment using the Sex Discrimination Act. While any woman contemplating a claim should seek legal advice from one of the agencies listed at the end of the chapter, it is easier to do this knowing something of the procedures involved.

Although no cases of sexual harassment have yet been heard under the SDA, the act has been used to pursue complaints with employers, particularly where no other remedy was available. In some instances, starting legal proceedings may be enough for the employer to take the issue seriously. A victim of harassment may find her case settled by the employer before the tribunal meets. If not, there is always the possibility of withdrawing the case before the hearing. It is always worth considering whether or not the law will help in a particular case, rather than continue to put up with serious harassment or leave the job.

The information in this section covers:

- qualifying conditions for claiming under the SDA;
- costs and legal aid;
- using the section 74 question procedure;
- application to an industrial tribunal;
- the role of the Arbitration and Conciliation Service;
- preparing for the tribunal;
- the pre-assessment hearing;
- the tribunal hearing;
- the appeals procedure.

## Qualifying conditions

**1.** You can only claim discrimination under section 6(1) and (2) of the SDA if your employer (together with any associated employers) has **six or more employees**. For example, if you work in a small office of three people, and your employer's partner has another office elsewhere employing four more, you would be able to claim. However, this size limitation effectively stops many women working for small employers claiming discrimination under just those circumstances where workplace organisation is weak.

**2.** You must file a complaint under the SDA to the industrial tribunal **within three months of the discrimination** taking place. Where harassment has occurred over a long period, the complaint should refer to **the most recent serious incident**. Even if you are unsure whether you wish to proceed with the claim, file the complaint. **You can withdraw it later**, but the tribunal rarely hear cases which have run out of time.

## Legal aid

**1.** Legal aid is **not available** to pay for representation at a tribunal. You may, however, be entitled to legal aid in order to obtain **advice**. The amount you receive, up to a fixed sum, depends on your income. You will qualify if you are unemployed. It is best to find a solicitor familiar with tribunal work, since she or he will know about the scheme. You are entitled to advice and help with letters, form-filling, collecting and preparing evidence.

**2.** If you do not qualify for legal aid, most solicitors run a **'fixed-term interview'** where you can receive half-an-hour's advice for a relatively small sum. Alternatively, a local law centre or one of the organisations listed at the end of this chapter will offer you advice, even if they cannot afford to take on your case. In seeking help, it is important to find someone with experience of sex discrimination cases. John McIlroy's *Industrial Tribunals*, also in the Pluto Handbooks series, contains useful information on how to prepare a claim.

**3.** Whatever the outcome of the hearing, **you will not normally be asked to pay costs**. However, the tribunal has the power to demand costs from you if it considers your claim was frivolous, vexatious or unreasonable. While this is unlikely, it is not clear under what circumstances sexual harassment cases might be treated as such.

## Using the section 74 questionnaire

**1.** Under section 74 of the SDA, you have the right to question your employer to find out why you have been subjected to unfavourable treatment. You do this using form SD 74, available from the Equal Opportunities Commission or your local Job Centre. The purpose of this form is to help you decide whether or not to take formal proceedings, so you can use the form **before you apply** to the industrial tribunal. However, to keep within the time limits you may need to file your complaint with the tribunal and then send the SD 74 to your employer. In this case it must be sent **within 21 days** of your formal application reaching the tribunal.

**2.** The questionnaire contained in form SD 74 may be useful in helping you decide whether or not to proceed with the case. You are asked to fill in a series of questions about the alleged discrimination which is then sent to your employer. **He is expected to answer your questions.** If he refuses or his answers are obviously inadequate, you may decide you have a strong case. You will also have some idea as to how your employer intends to argue against your case and whether or not your own evidence will be sufficient. When your employer receives the form, the

**seriousness of your complaint** may be understood for the first time. This could be particularly important where your employer has treated your reaction to harassment as a joke or is unaware of the actions of one of the employees. In this case **the form itself may be enough** for the employer to take appropriate action to stop the harassment, in which case you may decide not to take the complaint any further. You will have warned your employer of possible discrimination without having to make embarrassing and distressing statements in public.

**3.** A copy of SD 74 is included in this section, and has been completed to illustrate a **hypothetical case** of sexual harassment. The questions included will depend on the circumstances of the case, but it is important to include **only those facts which you want your employer to know about** and comment on. You should obtain two copies of the form, complete both and send one to your employer, keeping the other for reference. The form contains information on how to fill it in but the essential points are listed below. On the form, you are referred to as the complainant, your employer as the respondent.

**4.** The questionnaire should be addressed to your employer. In the case of a small workplace this may be an individual, possibly the person who is harassing you. In this case you may not want to send this form. You can still take a complaint to the tribunal without using form SD 74. In a large workplace the form should be addressed to the company secretary, managing director or any other name appearing on letterheads. In this situation the form is likely to be referred to the legal department. Where this happens the person harassing you may not be told about your complaint.

**Question 1.** You are the complainant so write in your name and address.

**Question 2.** Give brief factual details about your complaint (see example).

**Question 3.** This question is asking you to identify which sections of the SDA might have been broken by the treatment you received. Because the law is complicated it is **safer not to fill it in**, but to delete the word 'because'. You are entitled to do this.

**Questions 4 and 5.** These are questions the respondent (your employer) should answer.

**Question 6.** This space is for your own questions to the respondent. Their purpose is to get the respondent **to admit** that harassment happened and that this amounts to unfavourable treatment. You should not include information which you do not want your employer to know about or which he may be able to use against you. Try to get some help with this.

**Question 7.** Insert the address for the respondent's reply. This may be your own or you may have a solicitor who will handle the reply.

Remember to sign and date the form.

**5.** The respondent (your employer) **cannot be compelled** to answer your questions on the second part of the form SD 74(b). However, if you decide to proceed to the tribunal, this may count against him. Unless there is good reason, he is expected to reply within a reasonable time and to make the replies clearly and without ambiguity. When you receive the reply, you may find your employer agrees with some of your case but not all. Examine his answers and decide:

- if you agree with what is said;
- whether the answers given are relevant to your case;
- which replies are unsatisfactory or untrue;
- whether all the answers tie up with other information you already have.

Depending on these replies, you may or may not decide to continue with the complaint.

### Applying to the industrial tribunal

**1.** To make a formal application to the tribunal, **complete two copies** of the application form IT 1, available from your local Job Centre or Employment Office. If you cannot obtain a form easily, send a letter containing your name and address, the name and address of your employer and the grounds of your claim. Send one copy of the completed form to the Central Office of Industrial Tribunals (address at end of book). A separate form is available in Scotland. The form must reach the tribunal **within three months of the incident** you are complaining about. They should send you an acknowledgement within a few days. If the tribunal inform you that they consider your case is not within their jurisdiction, contact the EOC for further advice.

**2.** The questions you have to fill in on the IT 1 are relatively straightforward. A copy of the form is included in the Pluto Handbook *Industrial Tribunals*, by John McIlroy. In completing

THE SEX DISCRIMINATION ACT 1975 SECTION 74 (1)(b)

**REPLY BY RESPONDENT**

| | |
|---|---|
| Name of complainant | To .................................................................... |
| Address | of .................................................................... |
| | .................................................................... |
| Name of respondent | 1. 1 .................................................................... |
| Address | of .................................................................... |
| | .................................................................... |
| Complete as appropriate | hereby acknowledge receipt of the questionnaire signed by you and dated |
| | ........................... which was served on me on (date) .......... |

*Delete as appropriate

2. I *agree/disagree that the statement in paragraph 2 of the questionnaire is an accurate description of what happened.

If you agree that the statement in paragraph 2 of the questionnaire is accurate, delete this sentence. If you disagree complete this sentence (see paragraphs 21 and 22 of the guidance)

I disagree with the statement in paragraph 2 of the questionnaire that in

*Delete as appropriate

3. I *accept/dispute that my treatment of you was unlawful discrimination by me against you.

If you accept the complainant's assertion of unlawful discrimination in paragraph 3 of the questionnaire delete the sentences at a, b and c. Unless completed a sentence should be deleted (see paragraphs 23 and 24 of the guidance)

    a    My reasons for so disputing are

SD 74(b)

1/76

b  The reason why you received the treatment accorded to you is

c  Your sex or marital status affected my treatment of you to the following extent: —

Replies to questions in
paragraph 6 of the
questionnaire should be
entered here

4.

Delete the whole of
this sentence if you
have answered all the
questions in the
questionnaire. If you
have not answered all
the questions, delete
"unable" or "unwilling"
as appropriate and
give your reasons for
not answering.

5.  I have deleted (in whole or in part) the paragraph(s) numbered . . . . . . . . . . . . . . . . . . . . . .
    above, since I am **unable/unwilling** to reply to the relevant questions of the
    questionnaire for the following reasons: —

Signature of respondent . . . . . . . . . . . . . . . . . . . . . . . . . . . .

Date

THE SEX DISCRIMINATION ACT 1975 SECTION 74 (1)(a)

**QUESTIONNAIRE OF PERSON AGGRIEVED (THE COMPLAINANT)**

Name of person to be
questioned (the
respondent )

Address

To ...Samuel J. Smith & Co. Ltd.,.................................................................

of ...374-380 High Street, Bloxton............................................................

.............................................................................................................

Name of complainant

Address

1. I ...Maureen Evans............................................................................

of ...25 The Maples, Bloxton..................................................................

....................................................................................................................

consider that you may have discriminated against me contrary to the Sex
Discrimination Act 1975.

Give date, approximate
time, place and factual
description of the treat-
ment received and of
the circumstances
leading up to the treat-
ment (see paragraph 9
of the guidance)

2. On Thursday 9th December 1982, around 2.30pm I was
alone with Mr B. Jones, a manager in the finance section,
when he made sexually explicit remarks to me. He also
said that he could assist in my promotion if I would agree
to sleep with him. Following this incident I was upset and
had to leave work early. I felt unable to return to work
for a couple of days. This is not the only occasion on
which I have been treated in this manner.

Complete if you wish
to give reasons,
otherwise delete the
word "because" (see
paragraphs 10 and 11
of the guidance)

3. I consider that this treatment may have been unlawful because

SD 74(a)

This is the first of
your questions to the
respondent. You are
advised not to alter it

This is the second of
your questions to the
respondent. You are
advised not to alter it

Enter here any other
questions you wish to
ask (see paragraphs
12–14 of the guidance)

4.  Do you agree that the statement in paragraph 2 is an accurate description of
    what happened? If not in what respect do you disagree or what is your version of
    what happened?

5.  Do you accept that your treatment of me was unlawful discrimination by you against
    me?
    If not

    a   why not?
    b   for what reason did I receive the treatment accorded to me?
    c   how far did my sex or marital status affect your treatment of me?

6.  (a) Do you agree that at 2.30pm on 9th December Mr Jones
    made sexually explicit remarks to me and indicated he
    could assist in my promotion if I agreed to sleep with him?

    (b) Do you agree that following this incident I saw Mrs Brown
    my supervisor, and told her I wasn't feeling well, and she
    agreed that I should go home early?

    (c) Do you agree that I was absent from work for the subsequent
    two days, and that when I returned I asked Mrs Brown not
    to give me work for Mr Jones?

    (d) Do you agree that on several occasions complaints have
    been made by myself and other women in the finance section
    concerning the unpleasant behaviour of Mr Jones?

    (e) Do you agree that my work record and time-keeping are
    satisfactory?

* Delete as appropriate
If you delete the first
alternative, insert the
address to which you
want the reply to be
sent

7.  My address for any reply you may wish to give to the questions raised above is
    ~~the address set out in paragraph 1 above the following address~~

            D. Renfrew and Partners, Solicitors,
            96 The Hides, Bloxton.

See paragraph 15
of the guidance

Signature of complainant ........ *Maureen Evans* ..................

Date ..2nd January, 1983.................

**NB** By virtue of section 74 of the Act, this questionnaire and any reply are (subject to the provisions of the
section) admissible in proceedings under the Act and a court or tribunal may draw any such inference as is
just and equitable from a failure without reasonable excuse to reply within a reasonable period, or from an
evasive or equivocal reply, including an inference that the person questioned has discriminated unlawfully.

some of the questions, note the following points:

**Question 1.** You are asked to indicate the type of complaint you are making. For sexual harassment cases, write in **sexual harassment and sex discrimination** so that the legal basis of your claim is clear.

**Questions 8, 9 and 10.** It is important to include the correct information on pay and benefits since it will be taken into account when assessing compensation.

**Question 11. Leave this blank** because until some cases of sexual harassment are heard under the SDA it is not clear how best to present this information.

**Question 12.** Give brief factual details about your complaint. If you are sending form SD 74 to your employer, you should use the same statement in both. **Do not** write more than is required to show the basis of your claim since you may inadvertently say more than you can prove. Finish the statement with, 'I was discriminated against because of my sex.' If appropriate add, 'I was unfairly dismissed.'

**Question 13.** Applicable only if harassment has led to dismissal. In this case it is still safer to **leave blank**.

**Question 14.** Where harassment has led to dismissal, you will need to decide whether or not you want to continue working for your employer if your case is proved. **Reinstatement** means you go back to your original job on the same terms and conditions as previously. **Re-engagement** means you go back to work for the same employer but not necessarily to the same job. In cases of harassment, you may prefer to transfer to another section. **Compensation** will be paid if you do not go back to work for your employer.

3. If sexual harassment has led to dismissal, you are entitled to have **the reasons in writing** from your employer providing you have been employed **for at least 26 weeks**. If you have not received a statement, write to your employer, asking for the date and reason for dismissal, and the name of the person who took the decision. You should ask for this to be sent **within 14 days** of receiving your letter. If your employer fails to answer, inform the Central Office of Industrial Tribunals.

4. Providing the tribunal agree that your complaint is within their jurisdiction they will send a 'Notice of Appearance' (form IT 3) to the respondent (your employer). If the respondent fails to return the IT 3 he cannot take any further part in the proceedings. You will receive a copy of your employer's completed form.

Question 5 is the most important as it outlines **the grounds on which the respondent intends to resist your claim**. If you do not think sufficient information has been given you can write to the respondent asking for further details. You may, however, find it more appropriate to use form SD 74 to obtain the information you need. Remember, this can only be sent to the respondent **up to 21 days after** your complaint has been received by the tribunal.

**5.** The respondent can also ask *you* for more information about *your* claim. It is important only to present details which you can substantiate. Try to get help if you are not sure how to answer.

### The role of ACAS

**1.** A copy of your application form (IT 1) is automatically sent to the Arbitration and Conciliation Service (ACAS) and dealt with by a conciliation officer. ACAS will try to settle your complaint before it reaches the tribunal. The conciliation officer will visit you to discuss the basis of your claim. These discussions are confidential and information given **does not form any part of the tribunal hearing**. If you are interested in settling the complaint, the conciliation officer will act as a go-between for you and your employer.

**2. A word of warning.** It is the job of the conciliation officer to obtain a settlement if at all possible, not to judge the overall justice of your case. A study by Jane Gregory into the help given by ACAS to women claiming sex discrimination shows that many conciliation officers know little about the SDA and some may not be sympathetic to women. Very few conciliation officers are women. Because sexual harassment is not well accepted as a workplace problem, there is a danger that the conciliation officer will not treat your case seriously. He may suggest your evidence is insufficient and that proceeding to the tribunal could be expensive. To avoid embarrassing publicity your employer may be anxious to settle. You may find yourself under pressure to accept a financial settlement **without your employer conceding harassment to be a major problem**. Only you can decide whether or not to go ahead with the case and you should not be frightened into accepting a settlement. Try and arrange for someone sympathetic to be there when the conciliation officer calls. If you do not want conciliation, tell the officer at the first interview and your case will be forwarded to the tribunal.

**Preparing for the tribunal**

**1.** To date no cases of sexual harassment have been heard under the SDA so there are no precedents to indicate how the tribunal will conduct the case. It is essential therefore to be well prepared. The first step is to **write out a statement** to include:

- your name, address and age;
- your employment history, qualifications and experience;
- details of your current job;
- wages and hours you work;
- the management structure of your workplace;
- a summary of what has happened to you, with dates and times.

**2.** You need to collect **evidence** to support your claim. You can do this from documents, by calling witnesses, and using the information from the respondent contained in form SD 74 and IT 3. Some of the documents you will need to obtain from your employer. If he refuses to let you have them you can ask the tribunal to compel him to produce them. For sexual harassment cases the most important documents are likely to be:

- your contract of employment;
- your personal file;
- your absence/sickness record;
- your medical certificates or self-certification forms;
- workplace disciplinary and grievance procedures;
- copies of any complaints you filed about instances of harassment;
- any written record you have kept on instances of harassment;
- a copy of the SDA and any legal information relevant to its use for cases of sexual harassment.

Because your claim is being taken under the SDA you will need to show why harassment is sex discrimination. You need to put together some arguments similar to those discussed in the earlier part of this chapter. Once a number of cases have been heard which establish sexual harassment as sex discrimination this will cease to be necessary.

**3.** If possible you should call **witnesses to support your claim**. These could include:

- people you work with who saw incidents when you were harassed or to whom you spoke immediately after an incident;
- other women you work with who have experienced harassment from the same man who harassed you;
- people at work to whom you complained about harassment;
- people outside work who may be aware of the effects on you of harassment.

You may find some people reluctant to act as witnesses, where for example they fear victimisation from your employer or embarrassment at talking openly about sexual behaviour. You can ask the tribunal to order a witness to attend, but you should decide whether or not evidence given reluctantly will be helpful to your case. If a person was responsible for keeping your personal records or dealt with your complaint, you may decide their attendance is essential regardless of their attitude, in order to verify specific facts.

### Pre-hearing assessment

Regulations brought in in 1980 allow the tribunal to order a pre-hearing assessment some weeks before the full hearing of your case. The aim is to clarify the issues and to identify whether one side or the other is wasting time because they have no legal case. If this hearing decides your case is 'frivolous, vexatious or unreasonable', you will be notified in writing that continuing the case may make you liable for costs. Since sexual harassment is a new issue for tribunals, the circumstances under which such a ruling might be made are as yet unclear.

### The tribunal hearing

1. If possible, go to a tribunal hearing to see what happens. The tribunal consists of three people. The chairman (sic) will probably open by outlining what he considers are the main issues and the order in which evidence will be taken. In sex discrimination cases it is usual for the complainant to go first. Although you do not have the right to make an opening speech, you can ask the tribunal to let you do so if you think it will be helpful. It could be necessary where the chairman has not identified the main issues at the beginning.

2. In presenting your case you will need to refer to the rele-

vant documents and call your witnesses. Each witness can be cross-examined by the respondent and you should make notes of what is said. If you are unhappy about any of the points raised in cross-examination, you can re-examine your witness. Once you have presented your case it is the turn of the respondent. He too will call witnesses whom you can cross-examine. The respondent will try to destroy your case. He may try to show that you are unreliable or a poor worker. Because the complaint is of a sexual nature he might suggest you encouraged the harassment by your own behaviour or dress. Try not to get angry and be prepared to counter these allegations. At the end, each of you sum up your case.

**3.** In your summing up you need to show that sexual harassment has led to your employer treating you less favourably than a man because of your sex and that this treatment amounts to a 'detriment' (see p. 153). To refute your case your employer has to show that you were not treated less favourably, or that if you were it was not because of your sex. In deciding the case, the tribunal must consider:

- if the **principles** of the case represent a breach of the Sex Discrimination Act;
- if the **evidence is sufficient** to prove a breach in this case;
- the **extent** to which the employer is liable for the offence.

If they support your claim and agree that you have suffered sex discrimination, the tribunal will go on to discuss possible remedies.

## Appeals

**1.** A tribunal interprets the law in respect of a specific case. Complaints of sexual harassment heard under the SDA are likely to be judged differently by different tribunals. The only way to challenge the ruling is to appeal to the Employment Appeal Tribunal (EAT). You can only appeal on a point of law by showing that the tribunal made a legal mistake. This means that the EAT would rule on the principle of whether sexual harassment is sex discrimination. Until an EAT judgement is made on this question, individual tribunals are free to interpret the law in their own way. To take a case to appeal, it is essential to have legal representation. If a case is sufficiently strong, the EOC or NCCL may be prepared to bring the appeal in order to establish a test case. You must **appeal within 42 days** of the decision.

**2.** You can ask the tribunal to review your case again. This only happens if the tribunal staff made a mistake or new evidence is available; perhaps a key witness who previously refused to come forward is now willing to do so. You must apply for a review **within 14 days** of the tribunal decision.

## Making a claim for unfair dismissal

The practical steps in making a claim for unfair or constructive dismissal differ little from those for the SDA. Anyone considering a claim should refer to the section dealing with the IT 1 application form and work through the subsequent stages of the procedure, building their case around evidence for unfair dismissal. All tribunal hearings are subject to the same legal aid conditions; however, the **qualifying conditions** for bringing a case of unfair dismissal differ significantly from those under the SDA. To claim unfair dismissal by your employer, **you must**:

- have worked for that employer for a **continuous period of 52 weeks** providing your workplace employs **more than 20 people**;

*or*

- have worked for that employer for a **continuous period of two years** where your workplace employs **20 people or less**;

*and*

- work for **16 or more hours a week**; if you work between **8 and 16 hours a week** you must have **five years' continuous employment** with that employer; anyone working **less than 8 hours** a week **cannot claim**.

Since most dismissals occur in small workplaces and during the first year of employment, these conditions effectively leave large numbers of women without legal protection. The strict provisions affecting part-time workers also discriminate against women workers.

## Legal advice

The legal remedies available to deal with sexual harassment do not provide a suitable mechanism for tackling the majority of sexual harassment incidents at work. However, the law may offer some support for women who have clearly experienced retaliation but who are unable to obtain satisfactory redress within their workplace. In these circumstances it is **advisable to seek legal assistance** to cope with the technicalities of the law even where a case appears relatively straightforward. Of the total number of unfair dismissal cases heard by industrial tribunals, around 75 per cent fail. Sex discrimination cases have been even less successful.

Legal advice is available from a number of sources and the addresses of organisations mentioned in this section are listed at the end of the book. Women who are members of a trade union should **contact their workplace representative** about any complaint of sexual harassment as soon as possible after the incident. Trade unions will prefer to tackle the issue through normal workplace procedures; if these fail, however, they may decide to press a claim to the tribunal. Under these circumstances, legal representation would be provided by the union. If a workplace representative is unsure about dealing with the case, it is advisable to contact the union head office since many trade unions are in the process of developing policies on sexual harassment at work (see chapter 4).

The Equal Opportunities Commission was set up to develop and monitor policies related to the Sex Discrimination Act. The employment section provides advice on individual workplace problems associated with sex discrimination; any woman experiencing sexual harassment can approach them for information and support. If a complaint raises important legal questions, they may be able to assist with legal and financial help. They have produced a useful booklet, *How to prepare your own case for an industrial tribunal*, although its practical content fails to indicate the difficulties and overall lack of success at tribunals of sex discrimination cases.

Information and advice can also be obtained from the National Council for Civil Liberties, Rights for Women Unit. A number of harassment complaints have recently been referred to them and they have published a pamphlet by Sedley and Benn, *Sexual harassment at work*, which provides a brief summary of the issues. Like the EOC, the NCCL will support cases which raise important legal points. Rights of Women, a group of woman lawyers, offer support and advice to women with legal problems and will refer women to a sympathetic solicitor. A free advice session for women is available two nights a week; enquiries can be dealt with by phone, letter or in person.

Any woman unsure of how best to tackle a serious incident of sexual abuse at work should contact Rape Crisis, which was set up to support women who have suffered rape or other severe sexual assault. The group provides an opportunity for women to talk with others about their experiences. If requested, they will accompany a woman to the police station, advise on legal representation and go to court for the hearing. Over the years they have built up considerable experience of the way courts handle cases of sexual assault. Groups exist in London and many of the larger cities and run a 24-hour telephone service.

# Useful addresses

**BNA Communications Europe**

17 Dartmouth Street,
London SW1H 9BL
*Tel:* 01-222 8834

**Central Office of Industrial Tribunals**

93 Ebury Bridge Road,
London SW1W 8RE
*Tel:* 01-730 9161

*or*

St Andrews House,
141 West Nile Street,
Glasgw G1 2RU
*Tel:* 041-331 1601

**Cinema of Women**

27 Clerkenwell Close,
London EC1
*Tel:* 01-251 4978

**Criminal Injuries Compensation Board**

10–12 Russell Square,
London WC1
*Tel:* 01-636 2812

**Equal Opportunities Commission**

Overseas House,
Quay Street,
Manchester M3 3HN
*Tel:* 061-833 9244

**Industrial Society**

48 Bryanston Square,
London W1H 8AH
*Tel:* 01-262 2401

**Institute of Personnel Management**

IPM House, Camp Road,
Wimbledon,
London SW19 4UW
*Tel:* 01-946 9100

**National Council for Civil Liberties**

Rights of Women Unit,
21 Tabard Street,
London SE1
*Tel:* 01-403 3888

**National Organisation for Women's Management Education**

29 Burkes Road,
Beaconsfield,
Buckinghamshire

**Rape Crisis Centre**

PO Box 69,
London WC1 9NJ
*Tel:* 01-278 3956 (day)
*or* 01-837 1600 (24hr)

## Rights of Women

374 Grays Inn Road,
London WC1
*Tel:* 01-278 6349

## Spare Rib

27 Clerkenwell Close,
London EC1
*Tel:* 01-253 9792

## Trades Union Congress

Congress House,
Great Russell Street,
London WC1
*Tel:* 01-636 4030

## A Woman's Place

Hungerford House,
Victoria Embankment,
London WC1
*Tel:* 01-836 6081
(for details of local women's
groups, women in manual
trades, etc.)

## Women's Aid Federation, England

374 Grays Inn Road,
London WC1
*Tel:* 01-837 9316

## Women Against Violence Against Women

c/o A Woman's Place

# Bibliography

Aldred, C. *Women at Work*, London: Pan Trade Union Studies 1981

Alfred Marks Bureau, *Sex in the Office — an Investigation into the Incidence of Sexual Harassment*, London: Statistical Services Division 1982

Alliance Against Sexual Coercion, *Fighting Sexual Harassment*, Boston: 1981

Beale, J. *Getting it Together: Women as Trade Unionists*, London: Pluto Press 1982

Benet, M. K. *Secretary: An Enquiry into the Female Ghetto*, London: Sidgwick and Jackson 1972

British Society for Social Responsibility in Science, *Office Workers Survival Handbook*, London: 1981

Bularzik, M. *Sexual Harassment in the Workplace — Historical Notes*, Somerville, Mass.: New England Free Press 1978

Clarke, E. *Stopping Sexual Harassment: A Handbook*, Detroit: Labour Education and Research Project 1980

Clarke, L. 'Sexual harassment and the Sex Discrimination Act 1975', *New Law Journal*, 2 December 1982

Cockburn, C. *Brothers: Male Dominance and Technological Change*, London: Pluto Press 1983

Collins, E. G. C. and Blodgett, T. B. 'Sexual harassment . . . some see it . . . some won't', *Harvard Business Review*, vol. 59 no. 2, March–April 1981, no. 81203

Cook, A. and Campbell, B. *Sweet Freedom: The Struggle for Women's Liberation*, London: Pan Books 1982

Cook, J. 'Sex and socialism', *New Statesman*, 7 January 1983

Cooper, C. and Davidson, M. *High Pressure: Working Lives of Women Managers*, Glasgow: Fontana 1982

Coote, A. *Equality at Work? Women in Men's Jobs*, Glasgow: Collins 1979

Coote, A. and Kellner, P. 'Hear this Brother: Women Workers and Union Power, *New Statesman Report 1*, London: 1980

'Dilemma and decision: How should personnel director handle sex harassment complaint?' *International Management*, December 1981

Engels, F. *The Condition of the Working Class in England* (1st ed. 1892), London: Panther 1969

Equal Opportunities Commission, *Job Evaluation Schemes Free from Sex Bias*, 1982

Equal Opportunities Commission, *How to Prepare Your Own Case for an Industrial Tribunal*, 1979

*Equal Opportunities for Women in the Civil Service*, a report by the Joint Review Group on Employment Opportunities for Women in the Civil Service, London: HMSO 1983

Farley, L. *Sexual Shakedown: the Sexual Harassment of Women on the Job*, New York: Warner Books 1978

Gregory, J. 'Equal pay and sex discrimination: why are women giving up the fight?', *Feminist Review*, vol. 10, 1982

Harnett, O. 'Sex-role stereotyping at work', in Chetwynd, J. and Harnett, O. *The Sex-Role System*, London: RKP 1978

Kapp Howe, L. *Pink Collar Workers*, New York: Avon Books 1977

Kronenberger, G. K. and Bourke, D. L. 'Effective training and the elimination of sexual harassment', *Personnel Journal*, November 1981

Land, H. 'The family wage', *Feminist Review*, vol. 6, 1980

McIntosh, A. 'Women at work: a survey of employers', *Employment Gazette*, November 1980, pp. 1142–49

McKinnon, C. A. *Sexual Harassment of Working Women*, Yale University Press 1979

Miller, D. 'Men and trade unions: a case for positive action', *Trade Union Studies Journal*, vol. 4, WEA, Winter 1982

NALGO Research Section, *Equality? Report of a Survey of NALGO Members 1981*, Sociological Research Unit, University College, Cardiff, 1980

Pannick, D. 'Sexual harassment and the Sex Discrimination Act', *Public Law*, Spring 1982

Phillips, A. and Taylor, B. 'Sex and skill: notes towards a feminist economics', *Feminist Review*, vol. 6, 1980

Pollert, A. *Girls, Wives, Factory Lives*, London: Macmillan 1981

Read, S. *Sexual harassment at work*, London: Hamlyn 1982

Robarts, S., Coote, A. and Ball, E. *Positive Action for Women: The Next Step*, London: NCCL 1981

Rubenstein, M. 'When the office Romeo violates the law', *Personnel Management*, October 1981

Sedley, A. *Part-time Workers Need Full-time Rights*, London: NCCL Rights of Women Unit 1980

Sedley, A. and Benn, M. *Sexual Harassment at Work*, London: NCCL Rights of Women Unit 1982

Stageman, J. *Women in Trade Unions*, Industrial Studies Unit, Adult Education Department, University of Hull 1980

Trades Union Congress, *Equal Opportunities: Positive Action Programme*, 1982

US Merit Systems Protection Board, *Sexual Harassment in the Federal Workplace. Is it a Problem?* March 1981

Walsock, M. L. *Blue-collar Women: Pioneers on the Male Frontier*, New York: Anchor Press/Doubleday 1981

Whitbread, A. 'Female teachers are women first: sexual harassment at work', in Spender, D. and Sarah, E. *Learning to Lose*, London: The Women's Press 1980

# Index

ACAS, 176

advice: legal advice agencies, 180–2; for non-union workplaces, 59–68; for safety reps and shop stewards, 80–1; for union members, 81–2

attitudes to women: of employer, 30–1; of government, 36–7; of the law, 39, 164; of male workers, 40–53; of trade-union members, 37, 70–5

claim for damages, 165

clerical and secretarial work, 41–2

complaining: difficulties of, 22–3; how to, 63–5; to police, 163; via trade union, 78–82

counselling: within disciplinary procedure, 142; via trade union, 85

CPSA conference resolution, 75

Criminal Injuries Compensation Board, 166

criminal offences related to sexual harassment, 163

employer's liability: under Health and Safety at Work Act, 135, 161; under Sex Discrimination Act, 131, 155–6; in USA, 155–6

Employment Protection (Consolidation) Act (1978), 149, 157–60

Equal Opportunities Commission, 181

Equal opportunities policies, 134–5; as basis for negotiation, 102, 133; positive action, 53–5

Equal Pay Act, 35, 36, 39

films on sexual harassment, 124, 141

Health and Research Employees Association of Australia, 8

health and safety: effects on victim, 20–1; EMAS, 162; employer's policy, 135, 162; Health and Safety at Work Act (1974), 135, 161–2; Health and Safety Executive, 161

industrial action, 99, 103

industrial tribunal: applying, 170; cases heard under Employment Protection (Consolidation) Act, 158–60; cases heard under Sex Discrimination Act, 152, 153; preparation for, 177; tribunal hearing, 178; use for sexual harassment, 157

injunction, 165

legal cases: *Barnes v Costle* (USA), 152, *Bundy v Jackson* (USA), 154, *Corne and De Vane v Bausche and Lomb* (USA), 151, *Handley v Teddington Conservative Club*, 159, *Hurley v Mustoe*, 152, *Hyatt v Smithko of Salop Ltd*, 159, *Miller v Bank of America* (USA), 154, *Stevans v Powerflame Combustion Services Ltd*, 158, *Turley v Alders Department Store*, 153

management: involvement in campaign, 98; involvement in survey, 118; negotiating arguments, 132; policy statement, 133–9; training, 139–41; women in management, 10, 48–50 manual work: in factories, 30, 34–5, 46–8; service industries, 17, 42–4; women in manual trades, 50–3, 66

men: changing male attitudes, 85–93, 100; counselling, 85, 142

NALGO: branch newsletter, 126; Camden survey, 107–22; case involving NALGO, 78–9; composition of membership, 29–30; leaflet, 75; Liverpool survey, 107–22

NATFHE newsletter, 127

NCCL, 181

negotiations: management arguments, 132; over pin-ups, 102; trade-union arguments, 132

non-union workplaces, 59–60

nurses: sexual harassment of, 16, 44; support for, 66

NUJ, 75

pin-ups: campaign, 99–106; as sexual harassment, 14–15, 138

police: complaints to, 163

policies on sexual harassment: CPSA resolution, 75; in civil service, 137–9; National Labour Relations Board (USA), 136; TUC, 75, 76

press reaction: to pin-up campaign, 105; to survey, 117

press release, 117

private prosecution, 164

procedures: disciplinary and grievance, 63, 102, 141–5; handling complaints, 79–82, 141; to limit employer's liability, 156; for members, 81–2; for safety reps and shop stewards, 80–1; related to unfair dismissal, 158–60

questionnaire: analysis, 118; preparation, 116; purpose, 107; resources needed, 108; sample question, 112–16

Radical Midwives, 66

Radical Nurses, 66

Rape Crisis, 66, 182

retaliation: against the harasser, 48, 65; against the victim, 21–3, 62; by trade union, 103

sample agreements: disciplinary and grievance, 143, 145; employer's policy statement, 136; sexual harassment clause, 135

sample education materials, 89–95

sample leaflet, 129

sample newsletters, 126, 127

sample questionnaire, 112–16

schools: sexual harassment in, 44–5

SCPS, 84, 88

Sex Discrimination Act: employer's liability, 155–6; establishing detriment, 154–5; how to claim, 167; legal aid, 167; qualifying conditions, 167; section 74 questionnaire, 168; use for sexual harassment, 150–6

sexism: in job evaluation, 34–5; in job titles, 32; in language, 47, 72; in occupational segregation, 29–31; in part-time work, 38–9; and positive action, 53–5; and protective legislation, 31–2; in skill definitions, 33–5; in wage structure, 35–8; within trade unions, 70–5

sexual assault, 17, 163–6

sexual harassment: effects on victim, 19–21; cases, 13–18; in clerical and secretarial work, 41–2; by clients and customers,

43, 44; cost to the employer, 21; criminal offences, 163; explanation of, 23–5; in factories, 46–8; in management, 10, 48–50; in manual trades, 50–3; myths about, 18; in nineteenth century, 7; in nursing, 16, 44; outside the workplace, 43, 50; in schools, 44–5; in service industries, 17, 42–3; of students, 45; surveys, 9–13; by union members, 78–80

SOGAT 82, 75

stress, 20–1, 161

support: from co-workers, 61; from membership, 98, 100, 117; from trade union, 69–70; from women's groups, 66–7; lack of, 21, 43, 50, 52, 65

surveys: how to do it, 107–22; sample questions, 112–16; statistical evidence from Alfred Marks Bureau, 10, 11, 13, 19, 20, 21, from *Harvard Business Review*, 12, from NALGO (Camden), 10, 11, 19, 119, from NALGO (Liverpool), 10, 118, from *Redbook*, 9, from UN Ad Hoc Group on the Equal Rights for Women Committee, 10, from US Merit Systems Protection Board, 10, 12, 20, 22; of women managers, 10

TASS, 75

TGWU: case involving, 79; *Record*, 74

trade unions: action programme, 76–8; advice to members, 81–2; advice to safety reps and shop stewards, 80–1; education, 87–95; equal opportunities committee, 120, 141;

membership figures, 70; sexism in, 70–5; sexual harassment by members, 78–80; starting a campaign, 96–9; women-only meetings, 84, 123

training: assertiveness, 67–8; for management, 139–41; self-defence, 67–8; for trade unions, 87–95

TUC: *Charter for Equality for Women within Trade Unions*, 82–3; guidelines on sexual harassment, 8, 76; model equal opportunities clause, 134; positive action programme, 53; Women's Conference resolution on sexual harassment, 75

UCATT, 75

unfair dismissal: cases, 158–60; constructive dismissal, 158; legal definition, 157; qualifying conditions, 180

USA: affirmative action, 54; guidelines on sexual harassment, 24, 156; model policy statement for employers, 136–7; legal judgements on sexual harassment, 150–5

US Equal Employment Opportunities Commission guidelines on sexual harassment, 24, 156

Women against Violence against Women, 66

Women in Libraries, 66

Women in Manual Trades, 66

women-only meetings, 84–5, 123

Women's Aid, 66

women's centres, 67

Working Women's Institute (New York), 9

Jeremy McMullen

**Rights at Work** (new edition, 1983)
a workers' guide to employment law

Major changes in employment rights have been implemented by the
Tories. In this completely revised and expanded edition, Jeremy
McMullen takes stock of the current state of rights at work.

First published in 1978, this Pluto Handbook is the definitive guide
to employment law from the workers' point of view. It explains all
the individual and collective rights of working people, how to make a
claim, and using over 400 reported cases shows how the law is
interpreted and what workers can do for themselves through unions.

This book is especially written for trade union activists, shop
stewards, staff representatives and advice workers, but the
information is accesible to every working person.
*Industrial Relations Review and Report* said of the first edition:
'easily the most accurate, comprehensive and best written explanation
of employment law rights designed for union activists'.

Jeremy McMullen is a barrister and a London Regional Officer of
the General Municipal, Boilermakers' and Allied Trades' Union.

0 86104 739 3          paperback          £6.95

John McIlroy
**Industrial Tribunals**

More and more workers are having recourse to industrial tribunals,
seeking individual redress and maximum compensation; most shop
stewards and full-time officials will at some time in their lives be
involved in such cases. **Industrial Tribunals** is a timely guide and
textbook that is detailed, authoritative, accessible and comprehensive.
Its subject matter has never been covered before in such depth from
the workers' point of view. It will be essential reading for trade
union officers and lay representatives, for public interest groups, as
well as for the many workers who feel they might have a case but
would like to make sure of it before making the first moves. The
book will also be essential reading for management and for the legal
profession.

John McIlroy is staff tutor in industrial relations at the University of
Manchester.

0 86104 368 5          paperback          £5.95

Christopher Hird

**Challenging the Figures**

a guide to company finance and accounts

Christopher Hird's *Your Employer's Profits* (1975) quickly became a classic text for trade unionists wanting to interpret and challenge company accounts. **Challenging the Figures** revises, updates and expands upon that work to take account of current circumstances.

He deals with new accounting practices, the new legislation governing the form and presentation of accounts, and with the problems raised by recession and loss-making. The book explains how to understand the annual reports and accounts produced by virtually all business organisations: private sector companies, nationalised industries, building societies, cooperatives, and so on; how to get hold of information about them; how to uncover their investment strategies, their intentions, their state of financial health. Special problems in different sectors, whether nationalised industries or subsidiaries of large groups, are dealt with exhaustively.

A comprehensive manual for workers of every variety, their representatives and anyone — including managers — who feels the need to probe into the life and working of companies.

Christopher Hird is editor of the Sunday Times' *Insight* column.

0 86104 707 9          paperback          £5.95

# Other Pluto Handbooks

Michael Cunningham
**Non-Wage Benefits**

'a readable and worthwhile guide' *Daily Mail*  £3.50

Jack Eaton & Colin Gill
**The Trade Union Directory** (new edition, 1983)

'essential reference material for trade unionists'
*Labour Weekly*  £7.95

Maurice Frankel/Social Audit
**Chemical Risk**
a workers' guide to chemical hazards and data sheets

'an excellent guide for trade union safety representatives'
*Labour Research*  £1.95

Alan Grant
**Against The Clock** — work study and incentive schemes

'excellent and much-needed' *Labour Research*  £4.95

Patrick Kinnersley
**The Hazards of Work**

'essential reading for every shop steward'
*The Guardian*  £1.95

Dennis MacShane
**Using The Media**

'an excellent handbook' *New Statesman*  £3.95

Sue Ward
**Pensions**

'No trade unionist who is concerned with pensions can afford to be
without this book' *Labour Research*  £4.95

Sue Ward
**Social Security At Work**

'a cut above some of its cheaper contemporaries... a useful reference
work' *The Landworker*  £4.95

Pluto books are available through your local bookshop. In case of difficulty contact Pluto to find out local stockists or to obtain catalogues/leaflets (Telephone 01-482 1973).
If all else fails write to:

**Pluto Press Limited**
**Freepost** (no stamp required)
**The Works**
**105A, Torriano Avenue**
**London NW5 1YP**

To order, enclose a cheque/p.o. payable to Pluto Press to cover price of book, plus 50p per book for postage and packing (£2.50 maximum).